THE JEWISH CELEBRITY

Hall Of Fame

By Tim Boxer

A Shapolsky Book

For any additional information, contact:
Shapolsky Publishers, Inc.
56 East 11th Street, NY, NY 10003

First Edition 1987

1 2 3 4 5 6 7 8 9 10

Library of Congress Cataloging in Publication Data

Boxer, Tim, 1934-
JEWISH CELEBRITY HALL OF FAME

ISBN 0-933503-18-0

Book Edited and Designed by Malcolm Jordan-Robinson
Typography by Shapolsky Compositors

THE JEWISH CELEBRITY
Hall Of Fame

By Tim Boxer

Foreword by
Bob Hope

Introduction by
Steve Allen

Shapolsky Publishers
56 East 11th Street
New York, NY 10003

ACKNOWLEDGMENTS

For their invaluable aid, I want to thank Ken Kantor and Ward Grant of Bob Hope's office. I am also indebted to Broadway's premier agent, Milton Goldman of ICM, for his inestimable insight. For the days I spent in Hollywood interviewing the celebrities, I am beholden to the cordial staff of the Beverly Hills Hotel and the Beverly Hilton for their kindness and assistance in making this project a pleasure.

Several public relations people were a delight to work with, especially Ruder Finn's Marci Blaze and Karen Gee, Mike Hall, Terry Harold, Judy Katz, Mike Mamakos, Robert Palmer, Jeffrey Richards, Sheldon Roskin, Lee Solters, Jack Tirman and Sam Wall.

I am grateful to Danny Arnold, Jay Bernstein, Rabbi Shlomo Cunin of Chabad House, Jerry Cutler, Arthur Hiller, Milt Suchin and Bernie Wayne for enlightenment.

A special note of appreciation to Louis Auerbach, Jacques Bellini, Dean Blatt, attorney Leon Charney, Simon Cohen, Tommy De Maio, Alex Demetriades, Joe Franklin, Hadassah and Ben Futernick, Leonard Goldstein, Joe Greenwald, Arthur Lazar, my in-laws Norman (a descendant of the renowned Rabbi Akiva Eiger) and Kay Naham, Robert Parker, agent Arthur Pine, publisher Ian Shapolsky, Steven Silverberg, Miriam Soshtain Thurm, Jean-Pierre Trebot, executive director of the New York Friars, and Paul Zolenge for their support and friendship.

Finally, I want to acknowledge the help and encouragement from my wife Nina who made many suggestions and corrections. I thank my two sons, Gabriel the first grader and David the kindergartner, both of Yeshiva Dov Revel of Forest Hills, N.Y., for not taking too much of my time away from the typewriter to help them with their homework.

To my father Gabriel (z"l) who came with his brother Jack from the Polish shtetl of Czernica in Volhynia Guberneh, and my mother Annie (z"l) who came from nearby Kilikijow, and settled in Winnipeg, Canada, where I was lucky to be born.

CONTENTS

CONTENTS

Bob Hope with Tim Boxer while taping NBC's Bob Hope's Special *in Stockholm.*

FOREWORD

So what is a nice goy like me doing in a book like this? Well, for starters, I was asked. I guess that Tim Boxer wanted a gypsy's point of view.

And on the occasion of my seventy-fifth birthday, Alan King, on the stage of the Kennedy Center for the Performing Arts, made me an honorary member of the Jewish community, which entitled me to "twenty-five hundred years of persecution and guilt."

But most important, I welcome the honor to be between the covers with not only some of the greatest entertainers in the world but some of the greatest and most caring people in the world.

My one regret is that Jack Benny and Fanny Brice are not alive to be included in this fun-filled, roots-related entertaining journal. And what about Al Jolson and Eddie Cantor, Georgie Jessel and the teams of Willie and Eugene Howard, Smith and Dale, and the Marx Brothers, plus George Gershwin, Flo Ziegfeld, Arthur Rubinstein and Richard Tucker—all "talent roots"—and everyone in entertainment.

To show you where my mind is: Up until last week I didn't know that the three Bs of the arts were Bach, Brahms and Beethoven. I always thought they were talking about Benny, Burns and Berle.

To my good fortune, I have had the opportunity to work with many of the inductees to Tim Boxer's *Jewish Celebrity Hall of Fame*. But I have a tip for Tim: All of his subjects are candidates to everybody's HALL OF FAME.

Bob Hope

Steve Allen with wife Jayne Meadows

PHOTO:FRANK EDWARDS/FOTOS INTERNATIONAL

INTRODUCTION

Tim Boxer's idea for this book is truly novel. All of the planet earth's tribes are justifiably proud of their individual representatives who have achieved fame and/or distinction. Members of religious bodies, too, point with pride to such members of their flocks as have enjoyed notable success. But somehow this sort of demographic bookkeeping seems rarely to get into print.

In any event if any group has to start the ball rolling it's entirely fitting that the first to be so honored are the Jews. Comprising, as they do, a remarkably small percentage of the population of our nation they have distinguished themselves to a strikingly disproportionate degree. My own professional field, comedy, is practically a Jewish cottage-industry. Not only are scores of the funniest comedians and humorists Jewish but so is the even larger number of generally unheralded comedy writers who supply everthing from one-line jokes to full-length plays and films. Add to this the many Jews who have achieved success in the worlds of music, theatre, literature, science and public service and the list is truly impressive.

Although Jews number only about three percent of our population they have been awarded 27 percent of the Nobel prizes won by American scientists. "Jews are overrepresented in medicine by 231% in proportion to the general population," reports Dennis Prager and Joseph Telushkin in their *Why The Jews*? (Touchstone-Simon and Schuster). "In psychiatry 478%, in dentistry by 299% and in mathematics by 238%." Moreover American Jews are twice as likely to go to college as Gentiles.

Perhaps my own personal early background, a thoroughly anti-Semitic culture, enables me to perceive more clearly than most certain realities of Jewish-Gentile relations in the United States. Anti-Semites, whether of the truly vicious or almost casual type, perceive Jews as inferior. In my own case it took nothing more than attending a Chicago high school which had a largely Jewish student body to disabuse me of the stupid notion of Jewish inferiority. My point is by no means that Jews are no better or worse than the rest of us.

On the contrary, they are superior.

The family life of Jews, for example, has traditionally been remarkably stable. It hardly requires mentioning that Jews, as a class, are better educated than most of the Gentiles with whom they come into contact. And even though as a Christian I was raised in a culture which almost daily preached that charity is the greatest of virtues, I never saw the ideal properly and fully acted upon until I became aware of the inspiring generosity of American Jews.

In any event, along comes Mr. Boxer to provide a sort of Jewish Yellow Pages of high achievement. In so doing he has written perhaps the only book that will be of equal interest to Jews, anti-Semites and average readers.

As I once suggested, in a short story titled "The Day the Jews Disappeared," our nation would quickly sink into a long-term state of disaster if it were not for the ongoing contributions of the Jewish segment of the American population.

Mr. Boxer provides numerous specifics.

STEVE ALLEN

THE JEWISH CELEBRITY
Hall Of Fame

The author at work, photographing Jack Benny.

Superstars, screen idols, movers and shakers, jet set personalities and headline makers. These extraordinary people continue to fascinate us. We are insatiable for news and gossip of their careers and lifestyles.

I have been curious about them since I was a college student in Chicago, where I also was a police reporter for the City News Bureau and feature writer for *The Sentinel*, a Jewish publication. It was in the normal course of covering Rush Street nightlife for the *Near North News*, a neighborhood weekly, that I discovered an obscure comic named Dick Gregory desperately plying his trade at a student hangout, the Fickle Pickle. Impressed with his outrageously fresh brand of socially incisive humor—at my prodding, *Time* was soon to dub him "the Negro Mort Sahl"—I became his public relations advance man and road manager.

Greg admitted he was looking for someone like me to open the right doors to enable him to break out of the confining black ghetto clubs of Chicago's South Side, and explode onto the mainstream supper clubs and television variety shows. Through sheer publicity and word of mouth, I promoted Dick Gregory overnight (that is, over a three-month period at the Playboy Club) as the newest star sensation on the night club circuit.

Perhaps that is where my fascination with show people and their making took root. I turned my interest into a career of people watching, highlighted by seventeen exciting years as associate of syndicated columnist Earl Wilson of the *New York Post*. There was no greater teacher than the beloved "Oil," as his Brooklyn constituents called him. He was the greatest of the Broadway breed of celebrity chronicler. I was invited to celebrity parties at the Russian Tea Room, Sardi's, the Tower Suite, Regine's, the Waldorf-Astoria and the Milford Plaza. I went to film premieres and Broadway openings. I interviewed such personalities as Cliff Robertson, Walter Matthau, Lynn Redgrave and Eva Gabor, and shot pictures of many others, including Barbra Streisand, Johnny Carson and Xaviera Hollander, the Happy Hooker—and even Brooklyn mobster Joey Gallo at his wedding at Jerry Orbach's townhouse three weeks before he was gunned down in Little Italy.

When Earl retired, after forty glorious years of reporting the comings and goings of the show biz greats, I continued with *The Post* on the television beat. At the same time I specialized in covering news of Jewish personalities in a column called "Traveling with the Stars" for *The Jewish Week* of New York. I am eternally grateful for its former editor and publisher, the widely respected Philip Hochstein who, when asked if he'd like a Jewish version of the Earl Wilson column, immediately accepted my offer. The paper's current editor and publisher, Phillip Ritzenberg, continues to provide me with a berth to record the amusing anecdotes and gossipy tidings of Jewish stars.

With the phenomenal success of such personality oriented magazines as *People* and *Us*, the proliferation of people columns in newspapers across the country, the burgeoning business of gossipy talk shows on the airwaves as well as show biz segments on the evening news, my Jewish celebrity column began to flourish and appear in other papers.

Celebrities—you can read about them everywhere. But where do you turn if you want to find out more about the Jewish names that play so predominant a role in Hollywood and Broadway? That is what my weekly column, and this book, is all about. Meet your favorite personalities and discover their special background and unique upbringing. See how they struggled in a highly competitive milieu where fame and fortune became their new gods— until eventually many of them rediscovered their roots and embraced their long neglected heritage with renewed vigor and pride.

These men and women of distinction carry their Jewishness with joy (most of them), and in these pages, you will discover just what they think of their faith, how they relate to their brethren, what their relationship is to Israel and, simply, what it means for celebrities to be Jews.

The Mayor of Baltimore, William Donald Schaefer, told a Jewish visitor to City Hall, "I've always worried about what would happen if the Jewish community deserted the city and moved out into the country. Without the Jewish community in Baltimore, there'd be no cultural life here— no Baltimore Symphony, no Baltimore Museum of Art, no Walters Art Gallery—no nothing!"

His honor may be poor in grammar but he is rich in insight. His observation applies to almost every major metropolis. In searching for the foremost leaders in the arts and culture of America, one is constantly amazed at the number of prominent people whose origins are Jewish. There is a preponderance of Jews not only in show business. There are titans of industry and mavens of advertising, and, of course, Jews prominent in statesmanship and scholarship, too.

Jerry Herman remarked upon it. The composer of *Mame*, *Milk and Honey* and *Hello, Dolly!* exclaimed, "You know how amazing it is that, except for a handful like Cole Porter, almost everybody in musical comedy on Broadway have been Jews." I asked why that should be and he replied, "I think it has something to do with growing up in a Jewish home where there is melodic singable music. They all came from that atmosphere. I grew up in a home where there was always Yiddish and Hebrew songs." He added, "Cole Porter said when he wanted to be super melodic he'd put a Jewish melody in his song. An example is 'I Love Paris.'"

In the book, certain ground rules had to be established: Who to include?

Ron Samuels, producer of the movie *Iron Eagle*, which was filmed in Israel, and the CBS series *Downtown*, came away from his marriage to TV *Wonder Woman* Lynda Carter with a belief in her born-again Christianity. New York's most popular sportscaster, Warner Wolf, told the *New York Post* that while he is "proud to be a Jew" and a member of the Stephen Wise Free Synagogue, "I also believe in Jesus and that does not make me any less of a Jew than the next person." Let us also cite the case of a New York show biz character who is a closet Christian Scientist. Admittedly, this isn't cause for consternation in certain circles. I mentioned that he is a practicing Christian Scientist and got the response, "So what? I'm a Jewish accountant." Earl Wilson quipped, "I asked him why he didn't become a Jewish scientist."

Kirk Douglas, Lauren Bacall, Eddie Fisher and Suzanne Pleshette are among those who took non-Jewish mates. Hal Linden, the former Harold Lifshitz of the East Bronx, married a Catholic in the Community Church and raised his four children as Unitarians. But more about him later.

The criterion used here to determine who to include is the established definition of what constitutes Jewishness, derived from *halacha* (Talmudic law): Any person born of a Jewish mother or converted to Judaism.

There are more than a hundred names worthy of being inducted into the Jewish Hall of Fame. During these summer months I was able to interview only two dozen of these Jewish celebrities. Many stars could not adjust their busy schedules to meet with me. Others were away on film locations. Still others became suddenly inaccessible when their overly anxious press representatives reacted against the idea of a book solely on Jews. Many Hollywood personalities are still more interested in encouraging applause and admiration from the mainstream. A marvelous exception is Barbra Streisand who would not hesitate to produce and star in a film focusing on her heritage (*Yentl*) and is an admirable role model as a proud Jew concerned with the survival of her tradition (she gives substantial financial support to synagogues and schools).

But it all reminds me of Jan Murray's apocryphal tale. He entered show business expunging everything about his personality that might label him ethnic. He changed his manner of speech, adopted a different lifestyle, even changed his nose, and set out for fame and fortune as Jan Murray. One night, while starring in a posh supper club, a guy runs over and exclaims, "Murray Janofsky! Haven't seen you since you left the old neighborhood!"

One can only hope that, after enjoying this book, all those other Jewish personalities will respond to future interviews for induction in a sequel to *The Jewish Celebrity Hall of Fame*.

I prefer to think,
as in liberation theology
—if there are to be reward and
punishment,
they should be in this life,
not in the next.

ED ASNER

A recent near-death experience has imbued Ed Asner with a profound curiosity about the realm beyond this life. He passed out "from too much indulgence" and something happened.

"I was unconscious," he recounts, "and somewhere in there it seemed to me death took place, or something near death. It seemed beautiful to me.

"Because of that experience—which was like, it's not so bad—I am eager to find out if that experience was telling me the truth."

That is not to say Ed does not fear death. "I'm too smart to lose the fear," he insists. "We need the fear to continue to be productive."

But he is eager to find out what it is like after death.

Meanwhile this bushy-browed, compactly built character actor feels it is of utmost importance to concentrate one's energies in reaping reward for one's actions during a lifetime on earth. He believes man can aspire to God and eradicate inequality and injustice which man himself has created.

"The farmers in the Southeast are being boiled alive," he points out, referring to the deadly drought. "I hear that ten trucking companies are delivering hay from farmers in the Middle West to these hard hit farmers. That's how man marches upward from the swamp. God willing, if we last long enough, it's those kinds of acts that will free man from his shackles."

Ed is active in progressive movements. He is involved in Africa Tomorrow, an organization that initiates fish farming in African communities to offset further famine. He is trying to set up pilot programs in Arab countries. He presided over the Screen Actors Guild for two tumultuous years, often clashing with his more conservative colleagues led by Charlton Heston.

His two-room office, in a nondescript red brick building in North Hollywood across the road from Universal Studios of Burbank, is decorated with posters and photos depicting his interest in humanitarian endeavors, labor causes and Third World concerns. Among the mementos are bumper stickers proclaiming "Kill a Commie for Mommie," "Up Yours Coors" and "Boycott TWA." A poster heralds "Labor's Centennial 1881-1981" while another shows a little child in Nicaragua in the center of a rifle's target.

Why is he so obsessed with progressive ideals?

"The question is," he responds, "why isn't everybody involved?"

So what makes him such an activist for human rights?

"Though I find some Jews these days certainly lacking in Jewish soul, I credit a lot of it to my Jewish soul and Jewish awareness. Jews never knew when the blow would fall on them. So if we find some people drifting from that path, from that thought of progressivism, that thought of constant concern for human rights, then maybe they're feeling awfully comfortable and safe in America to be able to forget about the past so easily."

Ed credits his Jewish heritage for not allowing him to forget the unfortunate circumstances of people who need help.

"I don't know why every temple, every synagogue, every shul does not belong to the Sanctuary Movement. If the Sanctuary Movement had existed during the time of Hitler, many more Jews might have lived. I don't know why those Jews now living have not put that together. I guess they feel safe."

He quickly adds: "Certainly not all Jews. You will still find Jews involved in every progressive movement, and in goodly number. But it's the ones who aren't that amaze me."

His passion for equality and humanity for the underdog has its roots in the Jewish tradition of "Justice, justice shall you pursue" (Deuteronomy 16:18). He had a strict Orthodox upbringing in Kansas City, Kansas. He was born in a hospital on the Missouri side where most of the Jews lived. He was one of perhaps ten Jews out of a student body of two thousand at Wyandotte High School. He had two brothers and two sisters. His oldest brother would constantly get beaten up by his Slavic schoolmates.

Ed remembers when he had fights, too. He even had a physics teacher who told anti-Semitic stories. It didn't end there, of course. When he worked with John Wayne in the 1967 motion picture *El Dorado*, which was directed by Howard Hawks and co-starred Robert Mitchum, Wayne made a remark which didn't sit well with Asner. On the first day of shooting Wayne called out, "Where's that New York actor?" Asner had been in California five years, and "New York" was a euphemism for "Jew." He was once turned down for a part in the western television series *Bonanza* because the producer, a Jew, said he looked too Jewish.

Ed had it drilled into his psyche as a child to beware and be careful. His grandmother had sustained a broken rib in a pogrom outside Odessa. Lizzie Seliger, Ed's mother, came to Kansas City from Odessa in 1913. Morris David Asner, Ed's father, arrived in 1900 from Oshashek, near Vilna, Lithuania. He stayed in New York for a year, but since he was primarily a country boy, he went on to Kansas City where he had landsmen. He acquired a pony and a cart and went out collecting junk. Ed calls him a junkman, but when the family moved into a better neighborhood, his father was known as a scrap iron dealer.

A typical Jewish education ensued for Ed, who attended *cheder* after school four days a week, plus Friday night and Saturday morning services. Ed did not prepare adequately for his bar mitzvah. The rabbi had taken a vacation before the event. The big day was a major disappointment for his punctilious father. It was not until years later when Ed stood next to his own son, Matthew David, at his bar mitzvah at Stephen Wise Temple, that he felt redeemed from the perceived disaster of his own coming-out ceremony.

The biggest regret in Ed's life is when he opted to play football in high school on *Kol Nidre*. The idea was, in part, not to be too pronounced in one's differences in society.

"The coach said he needed me," Ed says. "I, of course, wanted to feel needed. I was seventeen. Mother helped expedite my getting out of the house and going to play.

"As it turned out, they would have won without me. I certainly would have been closer to a man had I obeyed God rather than Caesar."

His father had high hopes when his son went off to the University of Chicago. Ed was the youngest child. Neither of his older brothers became professional people. The oldest, Ben, who died in 1986, ran a successful stereo and record store in Mission, a suburb of Kansas City. The other brother, Labe, took over the family scrap iron business. (There are also two sisters: Eve, a social worker now retired in Los Angeles, who was head of volunteers at Albert Einstein Medical Center in Philadelphia, then administrative assistant at City Hall, and Esther, married to a professor of economics at Southern Illinois University in Carbondale, Illinois.)

Ed lasted a year and a half in college. During that time, he became active in college drama and made his stage debut as Thomas Becket in T.S. Eliot's *Murder in the Cathedral*. His first play also gave him his first love. She was a non-Jewish girl, and when his father found out he removed his financial support. Ed dropped his studies, gave up the girl when she proved unfaithful, but continued with the university theater.

Oedopus Rex was the next play Ed was scheduled to do. He called home to say he was going to stay on for a couple of months.

"If you didn't make it as a student," his father scolded him, "you're not going to make it as an actor."

"I'll be the judge of that," Ed replied.

That year, 1949, was a difficult time in Ed's relationship with his father, though "that was the only untoward thing he ever said," Ed notes.

When some of the best actors left the campus, Ed joined them in forming their own troupe called Tonight at 8:30. The first production, Yeats' *Purgatory*, was directed by a young man named Mike Nichols.

What followed was a short time of taxi driving and selling advertising in Kansas City and odd jobs in Chicago. In 1951 he was drafted into the Army and sent to France. During his two years of service in the Signal Corps, Ed managed a basketball team that became the second highest-rated Army team in Europe.

Discharged in 1953, he joined Paul Sills' Playwrights Theater Club in Chicago. Other members included Elaine May, Mike Nichols, Tom O'Horgan, Zohra Lampert and Barbara Harris.

Fortunately, Ed's father was able to come up to see him act once. He saw his son portray Rabbi Azriel in *The Dybbuk*. "He was pleased by what he saw," Ed says. "He never said, 'Go get 'em, guy!' He knew, no matter what he said, I'd keep trying my luck."

Ed came to New York in 1953 where, for two years and nine months, he played Mr. Peachum in the off-Broadway musical hit *The Threepenny Opera*, by lyricist Bertolt

Brecht and composer Kurt Weill (a cantor's son). Ed's father died during this time, in 1957.

When he was in a play with Jerry Orbach, he joined some friends for dinner at the apartment of Jerry's girl-friend one night and met Nancy Lou Sykes, a friend of Jerry's girl. She was a literary agent. It took two years for them to marry in a civil ceremony. She was an Episcopalian and Ed worried about the impact the marriage would have on his family. A rabbi converted Nancy and at the same time performed the religious wedding rites.

His Broadway debut came the next year, 1960, but the fulfillment of a dream ended in disaster. The play, *Face of a Hero*, starring Jack Lemmon, closed after forty performances. The dream turned sour, Ed turned westward and went to Hollywood. The rest is history.

He collected three Emmys for his portrayal of Lou Grant, the news director of a Minneapolis television station in *The Mary Tyler Moore Show*, which ran on CBS from 1970 to 1977. He earned an Emmy for the ABC mini-series *Rich Man, Poor Man* in 1976, and another the next year for a stunning performance as the captain of a slave ship in *Roots* on ABC. For *Lou Grant*, a CBS spinoff of *The Mary Tyler Moore Show* that lasted from 1977 to 1982, he garnered two additional Emmys. In total, he accumulated seven Emmy Awards. No wonder he is known as an actor's actor.

Besides his militant stand on social issues, Ed gives much of his time to charitable causes. He came to Boston to host a fund-raising auction for Maimonides School, an Orthodox learning center in Brookline headed by the renowned Talmudic scholar and Jewish leader, Rabbi Dr. Joseph B. Soloveitchik.

Although keeping kosher and laying *tefilin* were part of his early shaping, they no longer have meaning for him today. As a matter of fact, when *Forum* magazine polled celebrities, asking "Did you ever have a sensual or emotional experience that caused you to exclaim, 'That's better than sex!'" Ed responded, "My first pork tenderloin sandwich."

He elaborated to *Newsday*: "In Kansas, it was terribly difficult to procure kosher food. I remember one night when I went out with my older cousins, a brother and a sister, to the movies and then to a diner near the packing house. I got two pork tenderloin sandwiches on hamburger buns with onions. I took a bite, and it was ambrosia. I could have died for the elegance of that taste."

He identifies with the extended Jewish family.

"Growing up, we identified comfortably with Israel and the creation of a homeland, always talking about a homeland. Most of the time we thought it was a dream. It was part of the ritual. It's good to have a dream. The reality makes it much more difficult.

"I must say, when I lash out at something Jews may have done, or something Israel may have done, and the response comes back, 'What about what they did to us?', then I say, if we are doing this to be like others, what is the sense of being a Jew? A Jew to me is special, supposedly inspired to rise above the levels perhaps established for others. If we sink to the same levels, then to me there is no importance to being a Jew or any drive to maintain the identification."

Strong thoughts, but then Ed Asner is a profoundly opinionated, independent individual. Except when it comes to God, where he vacillates.

"There are times when I want to say I absolutely believe in him, and there are times I would say I am not sure what belief is. There are no atheists in the fox holes. I rarely, if ever, have been in touch with him or he with me."

He tries to keep in touch. On the High Holy Days he serves as a reader at the Stephen Wise Temple in Los Angeles. Throughout the year, he works tirelessly to uplift the spirits of the downtrodden and the suffering anywhere on this earth.

At the end, Ed thanks me for our conversation. "You made me feel good. You have a gentle manner. It's nice. It's enjoyable."

He points to a jar of licorice which we had been nibbling. "This is available to you at all times, even if you are just walking by."

Profile
Ed Asner

Given Name: Yitzhak Eddie Asner (named after Grandmother Etya).
Birthday: November 15, 1929.
Birthplace: Kansas City, Kansas.
Parents: Morris David Asner of Oshashek, Vilna, Lithuania, and Lizzie Seliger of Odessa.
Siblings: 2 brothers: Ben (deceased) and Labe of Kansas City; and 2 sisters: Eve of Los Angeles and Esther of Carbondale, Illinois.
Height: 5'8".
Weight: Do not publish it.
Eyes: Hazel.
Hair: What there is of it, fairly gray.
Education: Wyandotte High School, Kansas City; University of Chicago.
Marriage: Nancy Lou Sykes (1959), now separated.
Children: Twins, Matthew David, actor, and Liza Ellen, student at Northeastern University in Boston (b. 1963); Kathryn Leslie, student at Palos Verdes Marymount College (b. 1967).
Interests: Shell and rock hunting, gardening.
Personal Habits: Stopped smoking.
Clubs: B'nai B'rith.

PHOTO: TIM BOXER

Politics: Progressive Democrat

Social Life: Banquets and fund raising on the socio-political scene; otherwise it is dinner and a movie.

Exercise: Half-hour walk with 64 lb. weights.

Snack: Licorice.

Car: My 1976 Oldsmobile blew up on me, so I have a rental until I find a new car.

Favorite TV Shows: *Naked City, The Defenders, The Senator.*

Favorite Movies: *Paths of Glory, Fantasia, It's a Wonderful Life.*

Favorite Book: *Last of the Just.*

Biggest Mistake: Playing football on Yom Kippur in high school.

Biggest Irritant: Apathy.

Hero: The lay teacher, union leader, reporter in places like El Salvador.

Greatest Achievement: Being a good actor.

Vacation Spot: Caribbean.

Synagogue: Stephen Wise Temple.

Charity: Maimonides School, Boston.

Home: Studio City, California.

I never dared wear a purple shirt in public until I did **La Cage Aux Folles.**

GENE BARRY

The sauve, swank, sophisticated Gene Barry — the Jewish version of the dapper Cary Grant — started out as a chorus boy in a Yiddish play starring Menasheh Skulnick at the Second Avenue Theatre. He was sixteen and an inch over six feet tall.

"I was too tall and too skinny to fit in the soldier's uniform," he recalls. "The sleeves came up to my elbows and the pants came up to my knees. I was getting laughs and Skulnick was getting jealous. I almost got fired."

Gene learned Yiddish in his grandmother's house where he was born in 1921. It was located at 116th Street and Fifth Avenue in Spanish Harlem. The old lady insisted that all her grandchildren speak Yiddish. Gene was so close to her that he could speak *mama loshen* better than his three sisters and one brother.

Yiddish is the universal language of western Jews and transcends all boundaries. Thus his knowledge of Yiddish has helped Gene in his worldwide travels. When he toured South America for the U.S. State Department, Gene, who is not fluent in Spanish or Portuguese, was able to communicate with many people in the Jewish language.

However the man who was born Eugene Klass did not speak Yiddish in the show that boosted him to stardom as the dandy with a derby and a gold-tipped cane when he starred as *Bat Masterson* on NBC — during the years 1959 through 1961, but he was to establish himself as an actor with class.

His father, Martin Klass, was born in Zagare, a small town near Riga, Latvia; his grandfather had left Holland for the Latvian town where he married.

His mother, Eva Conn, was a Philadelphia native, whose parents had emigrated from Vilna, Poland where the family produced well-known scholars who had streets named after them.

Actually, Gene's father was quite some scholar and when he settled in the United States became a jewelry manufacturer in Greenwich Village, New York.

Gene's formative years were spent in a Brooklyn home saturated with Orthodox Jewish tradition and civic values.

Like so many other show biz hopefuls, Gene took the trek to the Catskill Mountains to break into the business. This was before his stint at the Second Avenue Theatre. He became the social director at the Majestic Hotel in Hurleyville, where he received the sum of $25 per week. Years later, he returned as a singer — yes, a singer — and was paid $15,000 for one performance.

At age 21 he made his entry into the Great White Way as the bat in *Rosalinda*. Shortly after that he joined another show, *Catherine Was Great*, at the same time the ingenue Julie Carlson was being fired because Mae West — the star of the show — objected to having another blond on the same stage.

The handsome Gene did not object to having a blond in his life, so when the show closed — and with it his role as the leading man to the flirtatious fifty-seven-year-old Mae — he proposed to the beautiful Julie.

"In those days, you didn't ask a girl to go on the road with you," he recalls. He was about to tour in a new play so, "I married her and took her with me."

Julie's real name was Betty Claire Kalb, and she hailed from the posh surburban community of Woodmere, Long Island. Her mother insisted on having her uptown rabbi officiate at the ceremony. On the other hand, Gene wanted his own rabbi from the old neighborhood shul, of 55th Street and 18th Avenue in Brooklyn, to participate under the *chupah*, too. That was Rabbi Sher, who had prepared Gene for his bar mitzvah at that synagogue.

The wedding was delayed until Gene's grandmother, Sarah Conn, arrived. The uptown rabbi, who had other appointments, couldn't wait, so Gene had the pleasure of his own rebbe performing the wedding.

That was in 1944, and the marriage has endured to this day. The couple is blessed with two fine sons and a daughter.

When Gene cocked the derby on his head and picked up the fancy cane to portray the dapper *Bat Masterson*, he joined an elite group of Jewish television cowboys that in-

Gene Barry and wife Betty at Tony Awards *supper party*

Photo: Tim Boxer

cluded Lorne Greene and the half-Jewish Michael Landon of *Bonanza* (1959-61 on NBC).

His Jewishness has never been a problem for him, but it has sometimes surprised his fans.

Betty once went into a store on Fairfax Avenue in Los Angeles to buy a *tallit* for their son's bar mitzvah. The owner took one look at the check and asked, "Are you the wife of Gene Barry."

When she nodded, he ran to the back of the shop yelling to his wife, "BAT MASTERSON IS JEWISH."

Following his years on TV as the fastest cane in the West, the industry honored Gene's class with an Emmy Award for his portrayal of the millionaire cop, Amos Burke, on *Burke's Law* (1963-66 on ABC). He followed this with the role of Glen Howard, the publisher of a *People*-type magazine on *Name of the Game* (1968-71 on NBC).

All these roles preserved his legendary image of the dandy. But his role-playing did not spill over into his home — where he was a doting daddy, even attending PTA meetings. Whenever he appeared too dapper, Betty was apt to call him "Mr. Cane" when Gene would tone it down.

From cowboy to cop to publisher, Gene has run the gamut of roles, but in 1983 he took on the role of a homosexual as the lover of a "drag" queen in *La Cage aux Folles* on Broadway.

"I never dared wear a purple shirt until this show," he says, laughing.

"It was a wonderful year. There is no place as satisfying to a performer, to stimulate the respect of the industry, than on Broadway. I chose to play a wonderful part. I don't condone homosexuality, but it's not up to me to tell other people what to do."

Betty, noting that her husband had played a psycho cop killer in the movie *Naked Alibi*, maintains, "An actor plays everything that's good. But you do draw the line. I'd rather see him play a homosexual than a child molester."

From such a long career, you can imagine how much memorabilia the popular actor has accumulated over the years. His house in Beverly Hills is bursting with cartons of press clippings, souvenirs, and momentos of a highly successful career as an actor.

"We started keeping a scrapbook one year," he says. "But when I got into films, I was in so many newspapers and magazines that I started filling up boxes instead of scrapbooks. I have the boxes stored in closets, rooms and in all the nooks and crannies."

Gene is now at the height of his profession, and the cartons crammed with clippings continue to creep into all the corners of the house. These are providing useful reference material now that he is writing an autobiography. He has 300 pages down so far, but he is only up to 1968. That was the year of Robert Kennedy's assassination.

On that fateful day Gene, who has always been politically active with the Democratic Party, had just come from Salt Lake City where he had opened a campaign headquarters for RFK, and was in the Los Angeles rally at the Ambassador Hotel--where he announced the arrival of their favorite Presidential candidate.

"Betty and I were both with him that terrible night. After what turned out to be his final speech — after he said, 'On to Chicago' — he turned to me and said, 'Thank you, Gene, for all your help.' Then he walked toward the rear exit.

"I was going to follow him, but at the last moment I pulled Betty back and said, 'We've been with him. Let's not go out with him the back way.' In that moment the shot(s) rang out."

Gene remains civic minded and is most happy to lend his name and energy to a just cause. He makes personal appearances for half a dozen charitable groups. He showed up at a major dinner for the Jewish Federation in Honolulu where a million dollars was raised.

Still, he yearns to be more involved in turning the tide of bigotry in our society. Norman Lear's People For the American Way or the B'nai B'rith Anti-Defamation League will find him a most effective spokesman for their program.

Profile
Gene Barry

Given Name: Eugene Klass.

Birthday: June 14, 1921.

Birthplace: Spanish Harlem, New York City.

Parents: Martin Klass of Zagare, Latvia, and Eva Conn of Philadelphia.

Siblings: I'm oldest of five—sister Jocelyn Manes of Dallas, sister Shirley Newman of Los Angeles, brother Julian Klass of Los Angeles, sister Reva Meredith of Matapouri, New Zealand.

Height: 6'1".

Weight: 185 pounds.

Eyes: Hazel.

Hair: Depending on what role I do, it goes from gray to brown and back again.

Zodiac: Gemini.

Education: New Utrecht High School, Brooklyn.

Marriage: Betty Claire Kalb (1944).

Children: Sons Michael and James; daughter Elizabeth..

Interests: Golf, writing a book on my life.

Lifestyle: Moderately affluent.

Personal Habits: Not neat at all. Wife, kids, maid took good care of me through the years, so I didn't have to be neat. But I'm getting better.

Clubs: Friars; Brentwood Country Club.

Politics: Democrat.

Car: Jaguar.

Pets: We raised golden retrievers. The last one died last year.

Ambition: I'd love to go back to Broadway. Having been nominated for a Tony for *La Cage aux Folles*, I'd like

*Gene Barry (**left**) kisses the hand of his co-star George Hearn in the* TONY-*award winning Broadway musical* **La Cage aux Folles.**

to win one some day. I'd love to get a part in a film that might be worthy of an Academy Award nomination. I'm still very ambitious in my acting career.

Exercise: I walk three miles a day on a treadmill at home.

Charities: Dozens, including United Jewish Appeal, Jewish Federation, and Vista Del Mar for children with behavioral problems.

Biggest Mistake: Becoming a cowboy on television. I didn't want a cowboy series. Of course, it made me a household name. But it damaged my career in that I lost the position I had in the film area and became a TV star instead. It put me in a pigeon hole, and I was never really able to climb out of that category. I was very active in films before, and I should have stayed there. I was tempted by the money and the role — the derby and cane turned me on. But it took me away from my major goal.

Biggest Irritant: Kids today don't seem to know about holding a door for you when you're coming behind them. No basic manners. That's especially so in New York, but I notice the same thing in Los Angeles. People are becoming less mannered, more intent on themselves. I was not brought up in an affluent home, but I grew up with manners.

Kosher: No, but I don't eat pork.

Jewish Education: Cheder at the temple in Brooklyn.

Synagogue: Stephen Wise Temple.

Awards: Man of the Year 1985 from ADL; Tony and Emmy nominations; Golden Globe.

Home: Beverly Hills, California.

George Burns and Gracie Allen

I write a book, sing, dance,
practice how to do the split,
kick the back of my head
—so when the time comes,
I'll have a good exit.

GEORGE BURNS

"You don't make any sense," Brooke Shields admonishes George Burns in the film *Just You and Me, Kid.*

"I'm not supposed to," he replies. "I'm a senior citizen."

Columbia Pictures threw a big bash at Resorts International in Atlantic City for the premiere of the film in 1979. Octogenarian George told how he had great fun teaming up with a fourteen-year-old nymphet to shoot the movie.

"We could only work four hours a day. The rest of the time was devoted to school. Then they'd let me out and I'd rush back to the set."

Ta dum! Seriously, George, how did you like working with a sweet young thing?

"I like young girls. I liked young girls when I was nineteen. I liked them then, why shouldn't I like them now?"

Rest assured, there was nothing going on between ol' George and our Miss Brooke.

"She was too tall," he sighed.

George is on a roll. He got his wind back in his eighties, flying high with his newfound success. The resurgence came about suddenly at age seventy-eight.

In the summer of 1986 I visit George at his office in the

Hollywood Center Studios. His manager Irving Fein, a proud son of Brooklyn, fills me in on some details of his client's career. Then the star pulls up in his brand new Seville.

A neatly dressed little old man shuffles in and cheerfully says "Hi" in his familiar gravel voice. His toupee planted firmly on his suntanned dome, his round black-rimmed glasses nestled on his nose, and his signature stogie perched in his mouth, George Burns settles into a director's chair beside his big oak desk.

"I just visited Gracie," he begins. "I just came from Forest Lawn. I visit her once a month. Talk to her."

His office, which he has occupied for thirty-five years, is spartan. "Same office, same carpet, full of cigar ashes on the floor. I don't want to retouch anything."

There are a few framed photos on the wall and little else reminiscent of almost a century of show business.

"Let me tell you something," he explains. "I'm not interested in anything that happened yesterday. I'm interested in what I'm going to do today and what I'm going to do tomorrow. I've got no memorabilia, no scrapbooks. I don't keep anything. All I got is what you see."

I saw a door in his office and wondered where it led. Irving says, "Open it." There was just a wall—with a poster of a *Penthouse* centerfold. What a gag!

George's second career as movie star, country singer and author began after his old pal Jack Benny died on December 26, 1974. Jack had signed to costar with Walter Matthau in Neil Simon's movie *The Sunshine Boys.* He succumbed to cancer before filming got underway. Irving, who was Jack's longtime manager and producer of his CBS series and specials, had a few months earlier signed George as a client.

"George hadn't worked in fifteen years," Irving says. "When Jack died, I put George in the film."

It was George's first movie since 1939, when he starred with Gracie Allen in *Honolulu.* He was nervous. He mentioned his bad memory.

He gives me an idea how bad his memory is. He had a

secretary named Jeri Beaujio. He used to take her to lunch all the time because she knew everyone's name. She had a great memory. She would say, "The man coming this way is so and so, the lady coming toward you is Louella Parsons." One day she nudged him and said, "The fellow coming your way is your brother Willie."

George remembered what Lynn Fontanne once said: "Learn the words till they tumble out of your mouth." That's what he did. Although he protested he could not act, he did not have to "act." He simply turned in a natural performance. His peerless portrayal of Al Lewis, the aging ex-vaudevillian in the *The Sunshine Boys*, earned him an Academy Award as Best Supporting Actor of 1975. The glitterati at the Oscarfest cheered as the oldest nominee ever took to the stage and declared, "I've been in show business all my life, and if you stay around long enough you get to be new again."

The born-again comedian first surfaced as Nathan Birnbaum on January 20, 1896, on the Lower East Side. His parents Dassah and Leo Birnbaum were extremely religious immigrants, as were most of the neighborhood. His father was born in Cracow, Poland; his mother, George thinks, came from Austria. They had never met until their families arranged their wedding in Europe. He was fifteen; she was fourteen. After two years and two children, they arrived in America where the father worked twelve hours a day as a pants presser. Needless to say, they were very poor.

The elder Birnbaum, a very learned man steeped in Talmudic lore, spent a lot of time in the synagogue poring over the ancient texts with his colleagues. He was the local *mashgiach,* an expert on kashrut.

"He made sure that everybody on the Lower East Side had kosher food," George explains. "Anybody had a wedding, a bar mitzvah, like that, he went to see that the food was kosher. Everybody had kosher food and we had nothing to eat."

There were twelve children — seven girls and five boys — living in a four-room apartment in a slum tenement on Rivington Street.

"On the Lower East Side," George notes, "everybody had a lot of children. That didn't mean that the Jews were great lovers. That meant it was very cold in that neighborhood."

If they were poor, little Nathan didn't think about it. The whole neighborhood was poor.

"The Feingolds lived on the corner, and we thought they were rich because they had curtains on their windows," George recalls. "I used to take their garbage and put it in our trash can and take our garbage and put it in their trash can so people thought we were eating well."

When the Italians had their religious festival in the streets, little Nathan would saunter over and eat their cookies. "I'd be Italian for two or three days."

Nathan would buy a cake of ice for five cents. He would split the block into four pieces and sell them for a nickel apiece. He had to pass through the Catholic neighborhood to get home. The Catholics and Jews would sometimes fight.

"When I walked through the Catholic neighborhood, they'd say, 'Are you Catholic?' I'd say, 'Am I Catholic? Are you kidding? My father's a priest.' And I'd run like hell."

George was only seven years old when his father died. He describes it poignantly in his autobiography *The Third Time Around*:

> I don't know what I expected, but I didn't realize it could be so quiet, so simple, and so sudden. It was a late Saturday afternoon, and my father was sitting in his rocking chair reading one of his religious books. My mother was looking out the window watching the kids dance to the organ grinder down in the street. I was on the floor playing. I heard my father call to my mother. "Dassah," he said, but she didn't hear him because of the music. "Mama," I said in a louder voice, "Papa's calling you." She looked around; his book had fallen to the floor and he was gone.

It was now up to her to raise Nattie and his brothers and sisters. "My mother was a great woman. She used to bring clothes into the house and she'd take out the threads. That's how she made a living. Very poor, very poor." All twelve children grew up as responsible persons. Their parents may not have been able to provide them with many material things, but they instilled in their brood a sense of dignity, pride, responsibility, and the difference between right and wrong.

Dassah was the rock of the family. George can't stop singing her praises.

"I'll tell you a story about my mother, a good story. My mother had a wonderful sense of humor. She didn't know she had a sense of humor—she just said things.

"I was in show business when I was seven. I sang with three other kids. We formed the Peewee Quartet and we sang on street corners, streetcars, ferry boats. We used to pass around the hat. Sometimes they'd put a penny in our hats, sometimes they'd put a nickel in our hats, sometimes they'd take our hats.

"I came home one morning—I was doing well at that time—and I had breakfast with my mother. And she said, 'You know, George, you come from a nice family. All your seven sisters were married virgins.'

"I said, 'Mom, the reason they were married virgins—they were all ugly.'

"My mother said, 'Pass the salt.'

"You see, my mother could handle any situation."

Mama Dassah proved she could even handle domestic strife within the extended family, when the traditional fabric of matrimonial bliss was threatened to be torn asunder. When one daughter talked divorce, Dassah sent for her. It was Mamie, married to a dentist, Dr. Max Salis.

"Tell me the story why you're getting divorced," Mama said. So Mamie told her. Mama listened, then she turned around and said, "Mamie, you're wrong and the doctor is right. I want you to apologize to Max. Tell him you're sorry and that it won't happen again."

Of course, Mamie did just that. Mama said so. The next day Mama sent for the husband. "Doctor," she said, "Mamie was right. Don't ever do that again."

The marriage endured. Mamie lived to be ninety-three. George called her up and asked, "How do you feel?"

"I'm ninety-three!" she snapped, and hung up.

George learned a lesson: Never ask anybody who's ninety-three how they feel.

When George was about to marry Gracie Allen, he wondered how his deeply Orthodox mama would react to a Catholic in the family. His mother wasn't well at the time; she was in bed. George said, "I'm getting married to Gracie tomorrow in Cleveland."

"Gracie's a nice girl," Mama replied.

"But, Mama, she's not Jewish, she's Catholic."

"If they'll have you, that's fine."

All the girls married within the faith, but not two of the boys. Isadore, who lives in Akron, married a Protestant. George married a Catholic.

"I was not religious, but Gracie was religious," George says. "She was a good Catholic. We had our two children, both Catholic, and their children are Catholic. My whole family—they're all Catholics. I'm the only Jew. I'm the only one who eats fish on Friday."

George never had a bar mitzvah. He doesn't know why. However, he wasn't too enthralled with religion. An incident early in life turned him off.

"What upset me was when my grandmother died and you had to have a *minyan* to pray. I don't know if I should tell you this story . . . but I will. You had to have ten people for a *minyan*. We could only get seven. The other three we had to pay. We had to pay them fifty cents each to pray or they wouldn't do it. That stuck with me all my life. I couldn't imagine anybody getting paid for praying."

He says he is not religious but he knows there is something—God.

"I have my own religion. I'm fairly charitable."

For his ninetieth birthday, George helped Cedars-Sinai

Medical Center raise ninety million dollars. Although he has never visited Israel, there is a George Burns Medical Center at Ben-Gurion University in the Negev.

"I hate to talk about what I do for charity. If you give to charity, you're very fortunate. What's so great about giving to charity if you've got the money?"

George counts his blessings for having met Gracie. "That was one of the big breaks in my life—that she married me. She was in love with somebody else then. She was in love with a fellow in New York, a very big star. I didn't look good in New York. I was a smalltime vaudeville actor. Out of town, in the small places, I looked bigger. So I kept her out of town."

Gracie, daughter of vaudevillians, was born in 1906, in San Francisco. The pretty Irish Catholic redhead left school at fourteen to join her three sisters in a singing act. She split in a disagreement over billing, enrolled in a secretarial school, and met George in 1923. He asked the unemployed singer to become his partner. Three years later she became his wife. They adopted two children, Sandra and Ronnie, and lived in a comfortable Beverly Hills mansion. They were inseparable until her death in 1964.

Eddie Cantor introduced Burns and Allen to his radio audience in 1932. The following year they got their own show, which lasted seventeen years. They made several movies, including *Big Broadcast of 1932* (and *1936* and *1937*), *We're Not Dressing* and *Love in Bloom*. They starred on television from 1950 until Gracie's retirement at age 52, in 1958.

George marvels how times have changed. "You don't have to be lousy anymore, starting out," he observes, "because if you're good, you make it very fast nowadays. I was very fortunate when I started because I was bad. I sang with the Peewee Quartet when I was seven. I met Gracie when I was twenty-seven. In those twenty years I did thirty or forty different acts and I was lousy.

"I worked with a seal, I worked with a dog, I did a skating act, I did anything to stay in show business. But I was a failure from seven to twenty-seven. I didn't think I was, because I loved what I was doing. I was in show business.

"I was bad. But I was very fortunate because the theaters were lousier than I was. I didn't develop until I worked with Gracie. I knew all about off-stage—exits and entrances—but I didn't know how to do it. I was able to think of it and Gracie was able to do it. That's what made us a good combination. Sometimes we'd finish the act and Gracie would walk off and I would follow and that's how I became a star. Believe me, it wasn't easy—sometimes I forgot to walk off."

For the kids entering show business today, George adds, success comes overnight. They go on Johnny Carson's *Tonight Show* and the whole world sees them. They become stars.

"Nowadays kids make it fast," George says. "They don't have to stay in business too long to make a lot of money. Like Peter Frampton. I worked with him in *Sgt. Pepper's Lonely Hearts Club Band.* His manager told me he made $52,000,000 in one year. He had one album that sold eighteen million. He got three dollars out of every album. Three times eighteen is what? I'm not a mathematician, I'm a country singer. It doesn't hurt to make $52,000,000. It's like the man who's dead, and somebody says to give him an enema. They say he's dead. And he says it can't hurt. It doesn't hurt to make $52,000,000, you know. Peter Frampton pays his manager twenty-five percent of his salary. His manager made more money in one year than Al Jolson made in a lifetime."

Cigars and Burns are a match. Ask him for tips on getting into the business and he will urge, "Smoke a cigar. When the audience is not laughing, keep talking. They're laughing, keep smoking. And if you talk while they're laughing, get into some other business."

Has anybody told him he smokes too much?

"Every doctor. The last few doctors who told me that are dead."

He smokes El Productos because they fit his holder. "I don't think it's nice for people to look at that wet end. I'm a very neat comedian. The nice thing about a holder: you can put a good cigar in a holder or an expensive one—they both taste the same.

"Milton Berle told me he spends two dollars for a cigar. Well, if I spend two dollars for a cigar, first I'd sleep with it."

There was a time, he says, when he used to cough a lot. Kept Gracie awake for years. Went to all the doctors. They all said the same thing: Stop smoking. He stopped smoking, but he was still hacking. It wasn't the cigars.

"Abe Lastfogel, head of William Morris, told me about a little doctor named Ginsberg, a throat man who had a dispensary in Los Angeles. He said go down and see him. So I went there. There were about fifty people sitting in the office. I said to the nurse, 'Tell Dr. Ginsberg that George Burns is sitting outside.' She came back and said, 'I told Dr. Ginsberg that you're sitting outside and he told me to tell you that he is sitting inside.' So I sat there until he saw the fifty people and by the time I went out there were fifty more. And I was hacking. Dr. Ginsberg looked at me and said, 'What's the matter with you?' I said, I keep hacking. He said, 'Why do you do that?' Then he said, 'If I were you, I wouldn't do that anymore.' So I never did it again."

As for savoring life in his nineties, the actor-comedian does not think old.

"I'd go out with women my own age, only there aren't any women my own age."

Actually he does have a female interest, Cathy Carr, and she is much younger than he. She is in the oil business in Dallas.

He told Martin Burden of the *New York Post*: "At my age I never felt better, never looked better, never made love better. And never lied better."

I tell George I intend to come back to Hollywood and interview him again when he reaches one hundred and twenty. "Why not?" he retorts. "I'll be here. I can't afford to die. I'd lose a lot of money."

George is a creature of habit. He has a daily routine he adheres to. He eats very little breakfast, very little lunch, but makes up for it with a very good dinner. This morning he had three prunes, two cups of coffee, no bread. For lunch he will go to the Hillcrest Country Club and have a cup of soup and half a bagel. He plays bridge with his cronies from one to three o'clock. "Bridge is a good game. It's complete concentration. It takes me away from show business, because all I know is show business." Then he goes to his house in Beverly Hills where he has lived for fifty years, and naps until five o'clock. He has a couple of martinis, and either goes out, or stays in and talks to Cathy on the telephone.

Does he intend to marry Cathy? He does not intend to marry anybody. He had one wonderful marriage with Gracie for thirty-eight years. How can you top that?

As far as dinner is concerned, it has to be simple because "I don't care much for food," he says. "For instance, steaks. I don't like a steak. A big piece of meat, you cut it and you chew it, and you cut it and you chew it. If you're going to work that hard eating, you ought to get paid for eating. Who wants to work that hard?

"I like hot soup. Food has got to be stove-hot for me. The reason for that is my mother. She said, if the food is hot enough, nobody knows whether it's good or bad."

He always comes back to his mother...and Gracie. They each serve as a constant frame of reference.

He says his mother was the greatest. One night she said to Sammy and Theresa, "I feel I've had it. I'm going to die." They said, "Oh, mama, don't be silly. Take your medicine."

"I'll take the medicine," she said. "And if I die very shortly, when George and Gracie come to the funeral—I know George isn't religious—let him sit *shiva* for half an hour. It won't hurt him."

Then she added, "Make sure the coffee is very hot. Because Uncle Frank, when he comes to the funeral, if the coffee isn't hot, he won't stay."

The next day, while George was working in Chicago, his mother passed away in Brooklyn.

When George reached another milestone, his eighty-fifth birthday, more than a thousand friends celebrated at the Beverly Hilton. The event benefited Ben-Gurion University of the Negev which named a building for the birthday boy.

"I'm going to go to Israel to see the George Burns Medical Center," he announced. "I hope they put my name up in lights. I might sing a few songs for the students and the white mice in the labs."

Dinner chairman Neil Simon read a telegram from a fellow actor, Ronald Reagan, expressing regret he could not be there as he had "a prior engagement with Chief Justice (Warren) Burger." Ronnie had his own *simcha*— Inauguration Day.

In the end, George says, he wants these words on his tombstone: "I'd like to be standing here reading it."

George Burns in Concert

★ ON GRACIE ALLEN: I kept changing names and partners until I was 27. Then I started to play in some good theaters, and people discovered I had a really big talent. They were right. I was married to her for 38 years.

★ ON HIS EARLY YEARS: When I was 18, my name was Harry Pierce and I did a singing act. There was something inside me that had to come out. And if you had something like that inside you, you'd want it out, too.

★ ON HIS CIGARS: I smoke from 15 to 20 cigars a day. At my age, I need something to hold on to.

Profile
George Burns

Given Name: Nathan Birnbaum.
Birthday: January 20, 1896.
Birthplace: New York City.
Parents: Louis Phillip Birnbaum and Dorothy Bluth.
Siblings: Brothers—Morris, Isadore, Sammy, Willy; Sisters—Esther, Sarah, Sadie, Mamie, Goldie, Theresa, Annie.
Hair: I wear a toupee. I don't think I'd wear one if I weren't in show business. It makes me look good. But my toupee is gray, it isn't dark blue.
Zodiac: Aquarius.
Education: Quit school in fourth grade.
Marriage: Gracie Allen, 1926-64.
Children: Sandra, a school teacher, and Ronnie, who breeds Arabian horses.
Interests: Bridge.

Personal Habits: I smoke cigars, drink martinis and visit a girl in Dallas.

Clubs: Friars, Hillcrest Country Club.

Favorite Book: Show business biographies.

Favorite Movie: The last one that's a hit.

Car: Seville.

Charities: Cedars-Sinai Medical Center, Los Angeles; George Burns Medical Center at Ben-Gurion University, Israel.

Snack: I don't care much for food.

Biggest Irritant: Stupidness, silliness, people saying things that can hurt your feelings, and they gain nothing by it.

Home: Beverly Hills, where he has a $2.5 million estate which he bought 50 years ago for $59,000.

Never got a dinner, but so what?
Eve — who told Adam,
"What do you mean, the kids don't look like you?"
— never got a dinner.

Red Buttons

He grew up in poverty in a rough neighborhood on the Lower East Side where "you either grew up to be a judge or you went to the chair."

The fact still amazes him that so many comedians came out of abjectly poor families — comedians such as Eddie Cantor and Jimmy Durante, to name just two. "There must be something in poverty that makes you see the funny side of life."

His hair always was red, but his name at first was Aaron Chwatt. A monicker as singular as that could only have originated on Third Street between Avenues B and C, on February 5, 1919. "Yes, I've been red all my life — my hair, not my politics.

"My parents were very kosher. As a matter of fact, we had one uncle who was a Jewish vampire. He wouldn't suck a neck unless it was salted first."

From age ten to eighteen he lived in The Bronx. "We came up by covered wagon in 1929. My father was wiped out in the crash — somebody jumped out of a window and landed on his pushcart." He had his bar mitzvah at the Bronx Jewish Center.

As a youngster he sang with the world renowned Cantor Yosele Rosenblatt. During the High Holy Days, little Aaron, an alto solo, was a member of Cooperman's Choir which accompanied the great cantor in the synagogue.

"I have all the cantorial tapes," Red said. "I ride in my Bentley in Beverly Hills and play the music. I stop for a light and people in the other cars look at me while I blast the cantorial sound on my stereo. It's nostalgia, I love it."

Show biz beckoned in his bar mitzvah year when he won an amateur contest at the Fox Crotona in The Bronx theater. He sang the overture until a truant officer from the Children's Society grabbed him and sent him back to school.

The carrot-topped, skinny kid answered an ad in 1935 for an entertaining bellhop at Ryan's tavern on City Island outside The Bronx. He was outfitted in a Phillip Morris uniform with forty-eight glistening buttons. Orchestra leader Dinty Moore dubbed him Red Buttons. He was sixteen.

That year his first paid job in the Catskills earned him a dollar and a half a week, plus room and board. It was at the Beerkill Lodge in Greenfield Park, N.Y., where Joey Adams was the social director and Robert Alda the straight man. Red went in as an alto, but his voice suddenly took a turn to baritone, so they made him a stooge. They did six shows a week during the season from July to Labor Day. "I got a buck fifty a week and I sent my mother a dollar every week," Red recalls. "With the rest of the fifty cents I went crazy—wine, women, sour cream. I went bananas."

He began singing, tummeling, joking and clowning in the hotels, resorts and nightclubs. "There's something in your own nervous system, in your own psyche, that dictates you need attention," he said, in explaining why one becomes an entertainer. "You enjoy doing it, you keep on doing it. I think you're born with it. If you stay with it, and you have enough discipline to make it work for you, you'll wind up in this business."

Like many other comics of his day, he paid his dues on the burlesque circuit, toiling for Harold Minsky. At eighteen he was burley's youngest comedian. He will have you know that burlesque is not a dirty word. Actually, burlesque, he says, is an old Latin expression meaning "Bring on the broads!"

He suffered his most embarrassing experience at the time. It happened at Minsky's show at the Gaiety Theater on 46th Street and Broadway. "The punch line of the scene was when the manager rips your pants off and you're standing there with bloomers, and a big lock on it with a question mark. One day I was late for work and forgot to put on the dress. He pulled the pants off and... there I was. Biggest scream I ever got in my life. I thought, I arrived...this is it...Nobody ever got a laugh like that. Until I looked down. Much to-do about nothing."

It was not all smooth sailing at first. Jose Ferrer, actor-producer-director, spied Red on the burlesque stage and offered him his first legit break. He was preparing to produce and direct a Broadway play, *The Admiral Takes a Wife*, an irreverent farce about Navy men having a good time at Pearl Harbor. Red went into rehearsals and everybody was set to open on December 8, 1941. As fate would have it, the Japanese decided to bomb Pearl Harbor the day before as if to prove that nobody really was minding the store. The show was cancelled, shattering Red's hopes for a Broadway debut.

The next year, however, Ferrer produced *Vickie*, starring himself with Red in a supporting role. So the comedian-turned-actor finally made it to the Great White Way, even though it lasted a scant six weeks. That same year he went back to burlesque in *Wine, Women and Song*, which turned out to be the death knell of burlesque in New York. The show lost its license and the city lost its runways. Burlesque, which had spawned such stars as Fanny Brice, Rags Ragland, Jack Pearl and Abbott and Costello, became taboo by official edict in New York.

Inducted into the Army in 1943, Red played in *Winged*

Victory, Moss Hart's tribute to the Air Corps. He was in the cast with John Forsythe, Lee J. Cobb, Mario Lanza, Peter Lind Hayes and Ray Middleton. He later also appeared in the film version.

Red has the distinction of being paid $1,000 for a single spoken word in a movie. He signed for a part in *13 Rue Madeleine* (1947), but before he arrived on the set in Montreal, the director gave the part to a local actor. As consolation, Red was put in a scene where James Cagney parachutes behind enemy lines. Red stood by the open hatch and shouted "Go!" as Cagney jumped. For that Hollywood paid him a thousand bucks.

His comic bent did not go unnoticed and he started making guest appearances on television. In 1952, CBS gave him his own variety show. *The Red Buttons Show* was a big hit for two years. Red jiggled around, clasped a hand over his ear and chanted, "Ho, ho, hee, hee, hoo, hoo, strange things are happening." Instantly it became a national fad. NBC picked up the show in its third year, but it was doomed. Writer after writer came and went, but the format floundered. Turning it into a situation comedy helped little in the ratings. It was canceled in May, 1955.

This high point in his career was now followed by two years of inactivity. It was the most depressing time in his life. Then came *Sayonara.* It was a casting coup similar in consequences to the chance the studios took on Frank Sinatra for *From Here to Eternity.* It was a long shot, but they took a chance on Red turning in a superb dramatic performance—for which he was amply rewarded. He received the Academy Award in 1957 as Best Supporting Actor. It made this little guy feel ten feet tall. That feeling never left him as he continued to perform in the best supper clubs and hotels. His lament as the man who never got a dinner in his honor is legendary.

Red discussed his professional philosophy over chopped liver at the Second Avenue Kosher Deli on the Lower East Side of New York. He was back in the storied neighborhood of his youth. "This is it," he kept saying. "It's like I feel no other place in the world, when I come down to the

Lower East Side. These days I never eat deli. I'm strictly into health food and vitamins. Here I'm cheating. I'm clowning. *Oy gevalt!*"

He remembered the time he used to hold court in Lindy's on Broadway. A child approached with paper and pencil, his mother in tow. The mother says, "Tell Red Buttons what you want." The kid was very shy and quiet. The mother urges him, "Tell Red Buttons what you want." Not a word. The mother nudged him again, "Tell Red Buttons what you want." Finally the kid says, "Ice cream."

Abe Lebewohl, the popular proprietor of the Second Avenue Kosher Deli, knew exactly what Red wanted and provided steaming matzah ball soup, the ultimate vitamin pill.

As a comedian, Red avoids ethnic material. "I don't do any of the Polish jokes. I don't believe in degrading any people. I think it's very dangerous. I don't like it, never did it. It was never my kind of comedy. When you're making fun of people, you're making of them something less than what they are.

"It's good to have a sense of humor. But all of us have our Achilles' heel. You gotta watch it with humor, because humor is very potent. Countries have been toppled, kingdoms have been toppled, administrations have been toppled with humor. Comedians are the MX missiles of society. No question about it."

Red lives in the ritzy section of Los Angeles called Bel Air with his wife and two children, Amy and Adam. He met his wife Alicia through mutual friends, at Danny's Hideaway, the posh New York eating place that was a mecca for show people in the sixties. The Puerto Rican beauty converted to Judaism when she married Red in 1964. Red helped organize a new Conservative synagogue, Temple Sholom. One Yom Kippur he sat next to Walter Matthau.

The comedian describes his neighborhood as very exclusive. "We have the Bel Air patrol. It costs me sixty dollars a month. They protect you against other patrols."

Profile
Red Buttons

Given Name: Aaron Chwatt.
Birthday: February 5, 1919.
Birthplace: New York City.
Parents: Michael and Sophie Chwatt.
Siblings: Brother, Joseph, in the hardware business in New Rochelle, N.Y.; sister, Mrs. Ida Feirstein, of Tuckahoe, N.Y.
Height: 5'6".
Weight: 130 lbs.
Eyes: Blue.
Hair: Red.
Zodiac: Aquarius.
Education: Evander Childs High School, The Bronx.
Marriages: Roxanne, burlesque artist (1940); Helayne McNorton, beautician (1949); Alicia Pratt Pagan (1964).
Children: Amy (b. 1966); Adam (b. 1970).
Interests: Reading, writing, thinking.
Lifestyle: Pseudo-Bronx.
Personal Habits: Health food.
Clubs: Friars.
Politics: Independent. Great friend of Hubert Humphrey.
Favorite Book: *Special Counsel* by Leon Charney.
Car: Bentley.
Pets: Two dogs, two cats, two parrots, two kids.
Ambition: Just to get funnier and funnier.
Exercise: Stretching, push-ups, exercise bicycle.

Red and Alicia Buttons at Friars Annual Dinner in New York.

Charities: Benefits for Israel and everyone, no discrimination when it comes to helping the poor and needy.

Biggest Mistake: Not going into show business sooner.

Biggest Irritant: Can't stand pompous people.

Hero: Simon Wiesenthal — authentic hero.

Bad Habits: I trust people too much.

Greatest Achievement: Surviving.

Vacation Spot: Home.

Jewish Identity: It's with me 24 hours a day.

Kosher: No.

Observe Holidays: Pesach, Yom Kippur (I try to fast, I try not to grab some *cholent*).

Synagogue: Sholom Aleichem Synagogue, L.A.

Jewish Education: The best — my mother and father.

Biggest Regret: Moving out of my cockroach-infested tenement on the Lower East Side, because they are getting $2,000 a month rent now.

Honors: Academy Award, Best Supporting Actor, *Sayonara*, 1957; Golden Globe Award, *Sayonara*, 1957; Star on Hollywood and Vine; N.Y. Television Academy Michael Award, 1953; Susie Award, Eddie Cantor Lodge of B'nai B'rith; L.A. Friars Life Achievement Award; N.Y. Friars Man of the Year Award, 1987.

Home: Bel Air, California.

Imogene Coca surprises Sid Caesar with an early morning cup of coffee on their TV show.

For a bar mitzvah you had
spongecake and a piece of
herring and a bottle of PM,
that was it.
You didn't spend more than
50-78¢.
You don't spend that kind of money.
If you made $20 a week in those
days, you made a good salary.
$25 a week, You got married.

Sid Caesar

Those were tough times when Sid Caesar grew up in the twenties in Yonkers, Westchester. His father Max, who came from Austria-Poland, ran the St. Clair Buffet, a neighborhood diner that catered to the European immigrant workingmen from the nearby hat factory or sign factory. His Russian-born mother Ida helped out at the cash register. His brothers worked there too.

"I didn't work in the restaurant," Sid says. His father said, "You're going to be different. You're going to learn. I want you to play an instrument." He came home from school one day and his father said, "Sidney, you're going to play the saxophone."

"Why?" Sidney asked.

"Because," his dad answered, "somebody left one here."

Sid learned to play sax, at fifty cents a lesson. He also picked up a little comedy shtick, free. The customers in his father's place would talk in their native tongue—Russian, Greek, German, Polish, Italian. As a five-year-old kid hanging out at the diner, he'd learn different phrases from the different ethnic groups who delighted in teasing him. The guys at the Italian table would tell him a wicked word in Russian and send him to repeat it at the Russian table. The Russians would tell him a bad Italian word and send him back to the Italian table with it. Everybody had a hearty laugh. Little Caesar suddenly found himself center stage.

After playing with a band in Westchester, Sid decided to try for bigger stakes in Manhattan. It took six months for him to transfer from the Yonkers musicians union to the major musicians union in New York City, Local 802. During that hiatus, he could not take a steady job with a band. So he got a job as doorman at the Capitol Theater for fifteen dollars a week.

"The previous guy quit and I was the only one who fit his coat," Sid says.

Each day Sid would take off his doorman's uniform, pick up his saxophone case and a notebook and go to Juilliard. He just sat in the back and listened, and learned about harmony, theory, orchestration. Nobody knew he was auditing the class. How else could a kid on a doorman's salary attend music school?

Soon Sid was playing with such bands as Shep Fields, Charlie Spivak, Claude Thornhill, and even as a two-week replacement in the Benny Goodman band. He did many gigs in the Catskills. His music career abruptly ended with World War II, when he enlisted in the Coast Guard, where his comedic talent predominated as he helped create revues. He appeared in the Coast Guard hit revue *Tars and Spars* which toured the country and became a movie in 1946.

What established him as a major clown in show business was *Your Show of Shows*, which ran on NBC from 1950 to

1954. It was followed immediately by *Caesar's Hour*, from 1954 to 1957. For eight glorious years Caesar reigned as television's most innovative comedian.

He was earning a million dollars a year. But his triumph on television took its toll. He could not sustain the intolerable pressure of six-day work weeks—without cue cards or laugh tracks, before a live audience. He sought solace in booze and soon also became addicted to barbiturates. Inevitably, the show suffered and the ratings dropped, causing NBC to cancel it in 1957. He became a has-been at thirty-five years of age.

He embarked on a twenty-year odyssey of living hell, suffering frequent blackouts on airlines and the occasional contemplation of suicide. At times he was near death from chloral hydrate and Scotch, the same lethal combination that snuffed out Marilyn Monroe.

In 1978 he was starring in Neil Simon's *Last of the Red Hot Lovers* at a dinner theater in Regina, Saskatchewan. It was a play he had done many times and he knew all the lines. This time, however, the accumulation of alcohol and pills befogged his brain to the extent that he fell apart on stage. After the first act, he collapsed in his dressing room. He could not go back on. He faced himself in the mirror, and for the first time, decided to choose between life and death. He was taken to the local hospital where he went cold turkey. He has been straight ever since, and is happy to be back among the consciously living.

When I drove into the courtyard of his fabulous Beverly Hills house, I met a virile, muscular, healthy-looking Sid Caesar at the front door. He ushered me though the house and out to the swimming pool. He sat in the shade and reminisced. He now eats only health food and exercises religiously every morning.

As a total skeptic, Sid cannot say that his religion played a role in his spiritual and emotional renascence. "How can I be religious? By putting on a hat, putting on *tefilin*? I did it before my bar mitzvah, but after that I was finished."

Every day after school, for eight years, he went to *cheder*.

"For eight years I learned nothing. Once I finished with that, I said, Boy, am I not going to go again!

"I learned *Breishis*, 'In the beginning,' *yeled* and *yalda*. That's it. The rest of the time I don't know what the hell I was talking about. Nobody ever explained it.

"You learned your *haftorah* phonetically. You learned to read the *siddur*. You didn't know what the hell you were talking about. Nobody explained anything.

"The fellow sat in the front with a stick and a schmaltz sandwich with a piece of herring, and that was it. 'You'll read next. You'll be next. You'll go.' That was going to *cheder*. That was the method of teaching. So you grow up and say, enough."

If his early Jewish education turned him off to a large degree, he still absorbed something that carries over into his late adult comprehension of life and the universe.

"I believe there are some very wise things in the Torah— they argue back and forth. But I don't think that anything that man has written yet comes anywhere close to what it is all about.

"I believe in something. I don't know if there is a God. I believe there is an energy, a force. Everything is energy and nothing disappears. The conservation law is at work.

"'There will be light.' If you want to believe that, fine. If it gives you solace, fine. I have nothing against religion. For myself, I believe there is something. But I don't believe any religion can say, 'Oh, we got a hook on it.'"

His son the doctor had a bar mitzvah. As for religion, Sid says it is up to his son.

Profile

Sid Caesar

Given Name: Sid Caesar.
Birthday: September 8, 1922.
Birthplace: Yonkers, N.Y.
Parents: Max from Austria-Poland, Ida from Russia.
Siblings: Three brothers: Abe died a few years ago, Milton died as a child, Dave survives in retirement.
Height: 6'.
Eyes: Blue.
Hair: Brown.
Zodiac: Virgo
Marriage: Florence Levy (1943).
Children: Richard, physician; Michele; Karen.
Personal Habits: No smoking, no drinking. I used to.
Interests: Physics, history.
Clubs: None.
Politics: Independent.
First Job: I played saxophone and clarinet in a band that got $1.50 for playing at a high school basketball game.
Favorite Book: *The Turning Point.*
Snack: Fruit.
Car: Cadillac.
Pets: Three dogs.

Exercise: Walk 3 miles every morning for an hour. Work out for 45 minutes. Then 35 laps in the pool.

Charity: Sid Caesar Foundation which gives to various charities.

Biggest Irritant: The indifference of people, people who don't care.

Hero: Albert Einstein.

Bad Habits: I got rid of them all.

Greatest Achievement: Learning how to appreciate life. Unfortunately, I came late to that. All the bad stuff is a "was." You forget about it; you don't hang on to it.

Biggest Regret: That I didn't learn all this sooner.

Vacation Spot: Right here at home. Vacation is where you want to make it.

Synagogue: No one in particular. I drop in anyplace.

Observe Holidays: On Yom Kippur I'd go to a shul just to say hello. On other holidays, I'd have some people over for dinner.

Anti-Semitism: When I was in the service.

Ambition: I'm writing another book, *How to Make Friends With Yourself.*

Home: Trousdale Estates, Beverly Hills.

Sammy and Tita Cahn.

I believe in the tenets of Judaism.
I believe in the law of Judaism.
I like the fact that most of the
Jewish religion is based on health.
Health is part of the Jewish
religion.
You wash before and after you say
hello!

SAMMY CAHN

Wall Street's most pre-eminent wheeler-dealer, stock speculator and prominent arbitrager, Ivan Boesky, keeps a midtown office on Fifth Avenue. You zip up to the thirty-fifth floor, pass muster by Henry Rausch, the chief security, and you find yourself in a maze of offices and cubicles reverberating with constant stock market activity on computers and telephones. At one end of the floor is the focal point, financial wizard Boesky's inner chambers. At the other end is a private sitting room, dominated by a grand piano, and displaying valuable art works. Adjacent to this cultural space is a small room, enclosed by glass, containing two chairs, a desk and an electric typewriter.

This is where songwriter supreme Sammy Cahn churns out his endless stream of songs. For years he had an office at the headquarters of Faberge, two blocks away on the Avenue of the Americas. He had a warm relationship with Faberge president George Barrie, himself a very talented composer. Barrie's high-tech office contained drums and piano, and he and Sammy would spend many hours making music. This team garnered an Academy Award nomination for the theme song for *A Touch of Class*, the 1973 film which Barrie produced. Glenda Jackson came away with an Oscar for her performance in it.

Sammy collaborated with Barrie not because he writes better music than composers Jule Styne (with whom he wrote "I'll Walk Alone" and "Time After Time") and Jimmy Van Heusen ("The Second Time Around" and "Love and Marriage"), but because "he smells better."

Sammy was forced to look for other working digs when Barrie left the company after it was taken over in a Wall Street maneuver by businessman extraordinaire Meshulam Riklis. Now Sammy is on the move again. Boesky is closing his Fifth Avenue office since being charged with illegal insider trading by the Securities Exchange Commission.

On his desk sits a framed quote by Mark Twain which was printed in *Harper's* of September, 1897. It is titled "About Jews" and reads as follows:

> If the statistics are right, the Jews constitute but one quarter of one percent of the human race. It suggests a nebulous dim puff of stardust lost in the blaze of the Milky Way. Properly, the Jew ought hardly to be heard of; but he is heard of, has always been heard of. He is as prominent on the planet as any other people, and his importance is extravagantly out of proportion to the smallness of his bulk.
>
> His contributions to the world's list of great names in literature, science, art, music, medicine and abstruse learning are very out of proportion to the weakness of his numbers. He has made a marvelous fight in this world in all ages; and has done it with his hands tied behind him. He could be vain of himself and be excused for it. The Egyp-

tians, the Babylonians and the Persians rose, filled the planet with sound and splendour, then faded to dream-stuff and passed away; the Greeks and the Romans followed and made a vast noise, and they are gone; other peoples have sprung up and held their torch high for a time but it burned out, and they sit in twilight now, or have vanished.

The Jew saw them all, survived them all, and is now what he always was, exhibiting no decadence, no infirmities of age, no weakening of his parts, no slowing of his energies, no dulling of his alert and aggressive mind. All things are mortal but the Jew; all other forces pass, but he remains. What is the secret of his immortality?

I asked Sammy: What is the answer to Mark Twain's inquiry?

"My answer might be a little naive," he ventured, "but I believe the Jew was destined to be immortal because of persecution and the constant desire to eliminate him. I really believe in my heart that if the Jews were left alone, they could very well lose that immortality."

Sammy, who has won the Academy Award four times ("Three Coins in the Fountain," 1954; "All the Way," 1957; "High Hopes," 1959; "Call Me Irresponsible," 1963) and one Emmy Award ("Love and Marriage," 1955), is very happy with his Jewishness. He believes he cannot be comfortable with any other religion. "The record of the Jewish contribution to civilization makes me very proud. I think the Jewish teachings are of a total charitable nature. I don't think any other religion is so involved in giving. It's part of the fabric of Judaism."

His favorite expression of his Jewishness is attending services on the High Holidays. He makes it a point to step into a synagogue on that important occasion no matter where he might be in the world.

He remembers standing in shul with his father. It was Yom Kippur and the entire congregation was beating its collective chest while reciting *Al Chet*, a long list of sins that one confesses, ranging from pride and scoffing to broken promises and robbery.

"I was fascinated," Sammy says, "that these devout men knew so much about sin that they could list so many of them. How did they know about this kind of thing?"

His father Abraham, whom Sammy remembers as a wonderfully warm, human man but devoid of humor—"I don't believe he ever made a joke in his life"—turned to his son and whispered, "I don't know why I'm beating my breast. I haven't done anything."

"I think that is so marvelous," says Sammy. "I think that is the heart of my father and the heart of Jewishness for me: Why am I beating my breast, I haven't done anything."

His parents came from Galicia, Poland, and raised Sammy and four sisters on Cannon Street on the Lower East Side. Sammy's story is the typical rags-to-riches saga.

Some people have suggested that a plaque be placed on the building Sammy was born in. As he puts it, "Not only did they not put a landmark on the building, but they removed the building, the street and the neighborhood. The entire area is now a vast housing project."

No matter. He went from Cannon Street to Canon Drive in Beverly Hills, where he has a luxurious house.

His father, who owned a restaurant, encouraged Sammy to be a doctor or lawyer; his mother Elka made him take violin lessons. He never had a chance to try for medicine or law, because he never graduated from Seward Park High School. "I hold the record for truancy there," he says rather sadly now.

So at fourteen, he went to work. He went from one job to another. "One summer," he relates, "my incredible mother arranged jobs for me. It seems she got me a new one each week. I didn't seem to be able to hold a job. I was an usher. I ran a freight elevator. I worked in a tinsmith shop where they made the square cans that carried film. I finally landed a job at the United Dressed Beef Corporation. Would you believe that the United Nations stands on the site of a slaughterhouse where I worked? When I quit that job I had to leave home! I slept on office floors. Finally I did go home for Passover."

He played violin in several bands and formed his own band with pianist Sol Kaplan, soon to be known as composer Saul Chaplin. Sammy started his songwriting career at age sixteen, with little success until he started collaborating with Chaplin. They sold several songs which were introduced by Ella Fitzgerald, The Ink Spots, Fats Waller and Louis Armstrong. But their big hit came when they adapted the Yiddish song "Bei Mir Bist Du Schon" into English. An obscure group, the Andrews Sisters, made it into a million-selling record in 1937, and everybody found fame.

When he started writing songs, Sammy Cohen decided to change his name as there was an actor named Sammy Cohen. Our Sammy became Kohn, but that was still too close to Cohen, so he changed to Kahn. There was a Gus Kahn, also a lyricist. So Sammy altered it once more, to Cahn. Interestingly, his son later on sought his own identity as a guitarist and changed his name to Steve Khan.

Sammy went to Hollywood in 1940 where he found a new partner, Jule Styne. Together they wrote many hit songs for Frank Sinatra, including "Saturday Night Is the Loneliest Night of the Week," "I'll Walk Alone" and "Five Minutes More." The partners' biggest success was the Oscar-winning "Three Coins in the Fountain."

Sammy and Jule created the score for the first multimillion dollar film musical, *Anchors Aweigh*, which MGM made in 1945 for the then unheard-of budget of two million dollars. The producers asked Frank Sinatra whom he wanted to do the score—Rogers, Kern, the Gershwins? Ol' Blue Eyes said Sammy Cahn. They said, Who?

Sinatra later sang many more Cahn tunes, such as "Come Fly with Me," "Come Blow Your Horn," "High Hopes" and "All the Way."

Sammy's two children are by his first wife, Gloria Delson, whom he married in 1945; that marriage lasted for eighteen years. Sammy has a grandson, Heath, from son Steve, and a granddaughter, Rachel, from daughter Laurie.

The proud father will never forget the unusual bar mitzvah his son had at the University Synagogue on the UCLA campus. Spencer Tracy stopped him on the MGM lot·and said, "I understand your boy's being bar mitzvahed. Could I come?"

Not only did Spencer Tracy come, but so did George Burns and Gracie Allen, Mary and Jack Benny, Tony Curtis and Janet Leigh, Dean Martin, and other luminaries.

Sammy was up there on the *bimah* beaming beside his Steven..His thoughts raced back to the time his own father stood with him on the *bimah* and handed over the tradition of Torah to his son. Now Sammy was handing it to his own son. It was very meaningful.

"I looked from the *bimah* and saw the faces of Edward G. Robinson, Jeff Chandler, Spencer Tracy . . ."

His one regret is that his mother did not live to get *nachas* (joy) from her grandson's bar mitzvah. It seems like Roosevelt not living to see V-E Day.

"My mother lived to see much of my success," Sammy says. "But that would have been her crowning glory. She was really into Jewishness. If we came to any neighborhood, if there wasn't a synagogue, my mother would start one, even if it was in a storefront.

He married his second wife, Tita Basile, in 1970. The man who conducted the civil ceremony is now a television star, Judge Joseph Wapner of *People's Court*. The nuptials were held at the home of the owner of the Beverly Hills Hotel. There were so many receptions at the Beverly Hills Hotel that people wished the marriage would last as long as the parties.

"Do you want me to convert to Judaism?" Tita asked.

"I have to be Jewish," Sammy replied. "You don't."

It lasted ten years.

"It was my fault," says a contrite Sammy. "When I realized it was my fault, I made it up to her by correcting everything. Now we live together and we're absolutely happy. One of these days we will remarry just to make all our friends happy."

Sammy is often called upon to write parodies for his celebrity friends at benefits and roasts. Here are special lyrics he wrote and sang on a New York radiothon for the Jewish National Fund on stations WEVD and WMCA. Sing along to the tune of "It's Been a Long Long Time," which Sammy and Jule Styne composed in 1930.

> I ask you all, to make a call
> The need is really great
> It takes a short short time.

> You mustn't fail, it's Israel
> And you decide its fate
> It takes a short short time.

> For eighty years you've listened every time we pleaded
> A shaynem dahnk for sending what we needed.

> My name was Cohen, so lift the phone
> The time is getting late
> It takes a short short time.

Profile
Sammy Cahn

Given Name: Shemuel Cohen.
Birthday: June 18, 1913.
Birthplace: New York City.
Parents: Abraham Cohen and Elka Riss.
Siblings: Sisters: Sadye, Pearl, Florence, Evelyn.
Height: 5'7".
Weight: 150 lbs.
Eyes: Brown and implanted because of cataracts.
Hair: Very sparse; once brown.
Zodiac: I don't believe in it!
Education: Look under hair: Sparse. Dropped out of Seward High School, but they gave me an honorary diploma years later.
Marriages: Gloria Delson, 1945-63; Tita Basile, 1970-80.
Children: Son, Steven Khan, and daughter, Laurie, both by Gloria.
Interests: Writing lyrics and doing for people.
Lifestyle: Casual.
Personal Habits: Typing whenever possible special lyrics for special occasions.
Clubs: Friars, board member of ASCAP, president of Songwriters' Hall of Fame.
Politics: Liberal Democrat.
Social Life: Entertain at my Beverly Hills house.
Favorite Book: *Gods, Graves and Scholars* by T. Ceram.

*Legendary songwriters Richard Rodgers (**left**) and Sammy Cahn compare notes at a New York Friars dinner.*

Favorite Movie: *Gone With the Wind.*

Snack: Cheese and apple.

Car: Chrysler New Yorker—because I wrote the special lyrics for the car and Lee Iacocca.

Exercise: Typing.

Favorite TV Show: All news programs.

Charity: Songwriters' Hall of Fame.

Biggest Mistake: Not getting a formal education.

Biggest Irritant: Our flawed political system which is still the best in the world.

Hero: All the great lyric writers before me, starting with Gilbert and Sullivan.

Bad Habits: Trying to make other people be like me (which they tend to be).

Greatest Achievement: My children and grandchildren.

Vacation Spot: My home in Beverly Hills.

Jewish Identity: I say a prayer every night, a personal prayer based on a Hebrew prayer.

Kosher: Not to the point of passing up an elegant meal.

Observe Holidays: All the important Jewish holidays.

Synagogue: I move about too much for one special synagogue.

Honors: Four Academy Awards and one Emmy. Only I and James Van Heusen have these.

Home: Beverly Hills; New York City.

Ed Sullivan (**left**) *welcomes emerging comedian Jack Carter to legendary* ED SULLIVAN SHOW.

My greatest achievement in life
was my son's bar mitzvah.
It was the only thing I produced
and liked. It was a big hit.
And it wasn't even on Broadway.

JACK CARTER

"I had to bootleg his Hebrew training," says Jack Carter about Michael's preparation for his bar mitzvah. The comedian was divorced from his second wife, actress-singer Paula Stewart. He had visiting rights with his son, who was living with Paula.

"I could barely get him out of the house," Jack relates. "All the time I was supposed to be taking him to dinner, I took him right to the rabbi, Joe Feinstein. He was also a comedy writer but super-Orthodox."

This went on for three years. All his visiting time with his son was spent with the rabbi teaching the kid how to read Hebrew and chant the *haftorah*, the portion of the Bible that he reads at his bar mitzvah. Jack just sat there patiently and waited.

The big event took place at Temple Beth El in Hollywood. Everybody came: Monty Hall, George Burns, Carroll O'Connor, Dick Martin, Don Rickles. "Rickles is very Orthodox," Jack says. "He can do the service with the book closed. He sent his kids to the Orthodox Hillel Hebrew Academy in Beverly Hills."

Even Paula was there. She was born of a mixed marriage —her mother was Irish, her father a German Jewish doctor. She did not appear at the glittering party that night at Jack's home where all the celebrities, augmented by Gene Barry, Cary Grant, Ed McMahon and countless others, celebrated Michael's coming-of-age.

Jack was exhilarated at the way Michael performed that morning. "He did it beautifully. He sang his *haftorah*. He wrote the speech himself. The temple president, Stanley Seidman, who is head of Nederlander Theaters, was so impressed."

While that personal event was his crowning glory, his biggest professional mistake was turning down *The Music Man*, the 1958 Tony Award winning show on Broadway. Robert Preston got the plum role and a Tony for Best Actor.

"I was studying and learning the part and working with the conductor of the show. I turned it down for a show called *The Carefree Heart*, a musical extravaganza with music by Leonard Bernstein, produced by Lynn Loesser, Frank Loesser's wife. It was in French and English, too ambitious. We never made it to Broadway. It closed in Cleveland. They just ran out of money. The big mistake was going to Detroit and Cleveland, where we thought we could escape the scathing reviews of Boston and Philadelphia. But Detroit and Cleveland were even tougher."

On stage in Atlantic City and Las Vegas, Jack is a bundle of nervous energy as he machine-guns his audience with gags and stories guaranteed to slay them.

Personally he is a perfectionist. He is a fanatic for cleanliness. He cannot abide dust. He loves to wash cars, clean houses, do the laundry, wash the dishes, and vacuum.

Sure, he even does windows. He is the role model of a state-of-the-art house husband.

His compulsiveness for cleanliness drives him to embarrassing situations. Invited to other people's homes, he will find himself checking china, running his hand on the bar to see if there is any dust, cleaning here and there.

"I like cleaning house—anybody's," he admits. "I clean counters in restaurants. I return all the trays in cafeterias."

Aware of Jack's compulsive habits, Lucille Ball was quite prepared when she invited him to dinner. Sure enough, Jack lifted his plate to check underneath. He found a note: "You shmuck, it's Wedgewood."

Above all, I found him to be a kind-hearted person and very considerate. Of all the personalities I interviewed in Hollywood for the *Hall of Fame*, Jack Carter was the only celebrity who came personally to pick me up. Everyone else (except Keith Gordon) expected me to drive to their office, studio or home. My rented Nissan got me there in every instance, even the few times I got lost in the winding streets. Beverly Hills cops are quite cordial and helpful and pointed me in the right direction each time.

During the week I stayed at the beautiful Beverly Hills Hotel, Jack came to call for me in his Mercedes with license plate JAC CAR. On the way to his house on Chevy Chase Drive, he gave me a tour of the neighborhood, pointing out such landmarks as Lucille Ball's house, Jack Warner's vacant estate, Elvis Presley's old mansion, and Jack's neighbor, Leonard Goldberg, in the house formerly occupied by Neil Diamond.

We sat in the sun-room, dominated by a bar, decorated with flowered wallpaper. The rest of the house was covered with paintings and antiques. His hobby is redecorating expensive houses in Beverly Hills and Bel Air and selling them at profit. The trees in his garden yield oranges, lemons and strawberries.

His father Harry Chakrin was eleven when he left Russia and arrived at Ellis Island. A stranger said he was from the Hebrew Immigrant Aid Society and would take care of him. The impostor took Harry's money and disappeared. The kid stood there in tears. Finally, the real people from HIAS came and brought him to his sister's home.

Jack was born in the Brighton Beach section of Brooklyn where his father ran a candy store under the El. A block away, the Brighton Beach Theater presented the greatest vaudeville acts, and they used to come to the candy store. Al Jolson, George Jessel, Eddie Cantor and Harry Houdini starred there.

"I used to run with newspapers and sell soda on the beach and hide from the cops under the train station," Jack recalls fondly.

He had his bar mitzvah at Amshe Emet, a little tin temple on Sea Breeze Avenue. When the women threw candies down on his head after he made the blessings over his portion of the Torah, Jack scrambled with the other kids to grab a bigger share.

"I was going to bring the candy back to the store. It was a shame. We should sell it. Even then I was saving, not realizing it came from our store anyway."

When the family moved to Bensonhurst, Jack attended the 75th Street Shul and Hebrew school. He was in the choir. Just before the High Holidays, his voice changed. All that rehearsal for nothing!

Show business got into his blood when he performed in a production of *Cyarno de Bergerac* at New Utrech High School. He became a commercial artist and would drag his sketches around, but to no avail. Someone suggested he audition for a scholarship at the Feagin Drama School at Radio City. He did his role of Cyrano and got into the school, which became the American Academy of Dramatic Arts. He met Jeff Chandler, also a scholarship student, and Sheila MacRae, and they became lifelong friends.

"Jeff, whose real name was Ira Grossel of Brooklyn, was a great artist," Jack says. "He was a pro commercial artist. He had a real portfolio. He sketched like Milt Caniff and did illustrations and cartoons. I just had a few sketchy things. I said if he couldn't make it as an artist, then I'll it up too and go into acting. Now I just do it for a hobby. I sketch on tablecloths."

When the three of them left the drama school, they went to the Milltown Playhouse in Roslyn, Long Island, to do Christopher Morley's play *The Trojan Horse.* Jack played a Nubian slave. During rehearsals he would clown around. The producer noticed, and told Jack he should not be wasting his comedy talent. He took Jack into Manhattan and introduced him to an agent. Jack was on his way as an impressionist.

One of his first jobs was a one-nighter at a hotel owned by Rudy Vallee's father in Poland Springs, Maine. Even while other performers were breaking in their acts or starting out in the Catskills, Jack was playing the major hotels in the elegant WASP vacation places, such as Poland Springs and Saratoga, New York.

Fred Allen heard of Jack's impressions and put him on his radio show at the height of its popularity. "It was a great thrill for me as a kid to meet Fred Allen," Jack says.

The big break, he says, came one summer when Rudy Vallee's manager got Jack a job for the season at a resort in Lake Tarlton, New Hampshire. People like Moss Hart, George Kaufman and Kitty Carlisle would come up for a Seven Lively Arts series of plays.

"I was fired the first night," Jack says. "The owner, Walter Jacobs, thought I was too dirty, too raw. I begged and screamed I'd change. So I stayed the whole summer.

"Years later I would always stay at his Tarlton in Miami Beach. The Ritz Brothers, Sophie Tucker, Al Jolson and Walter Winchell all stayed there. It's now the Crown Hotel."

Two days after our meeting, Jack tools up in his sporty Mercedes to the red-carpeted front door of the palmy pink palace, the Beverly Hills Hotel, and picks me up again. This time it is lunch at the prestigious Friars Club.

Jack is fuming. "I want to fire my agent," he says. "He's screwing me around. All the TV shows are now filming and he can't get me a day's work. I can't find him to fire him!"

That agent could teach David Copperfield a neat trick — how to make yourself disappear.

Jack tells me about his service during World War II. In 1941 he was drafted into the Army's Medical Supply Corps. When he was about to be shipped overseas, he was transferred to the Air Corps and wound up in a flying variety show with a big band. They flew in three bombers doing Red Cross and War Bond shows.

At one point, when his medical unit was attached to Patton's corps, he had a run-in with the general.

"I had just gotten out of a tank. It was a hot and dirty street, one hundred and forty degrees in the desert, and by this time you don't salute anymore. You were in fatigues and feeling filthy. Somebody grabbed my shoulder and spun me around."

It was Patton.

"Young man," he barked, "don't you believe in saluting officers?"

"Yes, sir."

"Well, salute me now, dammit!"

Jack saluted smartly and the general strode off, satisfied.

"I thought he was going to smack me or hit me with that stick," Jack says.

Once out of the Army, within eight months he was playing Loews State and Capitol Theaters in New York. NBC gave him his own hour, *The Jack Carter Show,* which aired live on Saturday nights in 1950-51.

He fondly remembers playing with Molly Picon at the Tic Toc Club in Montreal. Her husband's name was Yankel, same as Jack's.

"In Jewish culture, she is the greatest. She does a whole number on Jewish conjugation of verbs: *Gross, gresserer, a bulvahn, Klein, kleinerer, a peecheeyoonchekel.*"

Jack Carter's Cream of Wit

*I flew People Express. That's where, ten minutes before takeoff, all the passengers get together and elect a pilot

*Las Vegas is the only place where you can have a good time without enjoying yourself.

*I toured with Dolly Parton. She's overseas now, breast-feeding Ethiopia.

*Marriage is still the Number One cause of divorce.

Profile
Jack Carter

Given Name: Jack Chakrin.
Birthday: June 24, 1923.
Birthplace: Brooklyn.
Parents: Harry and Anna Chakrin.
Siblings: Two sisters: Sylvia manages Jeff's An Affair With Flowers in Los Angeles; Betty lives in Florida.
Height: 5'10".
Weight: 185 lbs.
Eyes: Blue.
Hair: Whatever I color it. Used to be brown.
Zodia: Cancer.
Education: New Utrecht High School, Brooklyn; American Academy of Dramatic Arts, Manhattan.
Marriages: Joan Mann (1951-54); Paula Stewart (1960-67); Roxanne Stone (1971), now separated.
Children: Michael (b. 1966) from Paula Stewart.
Lifestyle: Used to be flamboyant, out every night, frightened to death if I missed a party. My values have changed. Can't run anymore.
Clubs: Thalians, Friars, Vikings, Cellar Club.
Politics: Unenthused Democrat.
Favorite Book: *The Source* by James Michener. It amazes me that a Gentile can write so fulfillingly and

knowledgeably about Jewish history. I love that book.
I'm now collecting books on Jewish history and Jewish
humor.

Favorite Movie: *Dead End*, because when I first came here
I got to know the Dead End Kids.

Favorite TV Show: Milton Berle's show. I always patterned
myself after him, not working the same way, just that
enthusiasm, that energy, that brightness.

Snack: The hard end of a salami. There's nothing like a
nickel a shtickel. I had one at Nate & Al's. Now, that
nickel a shtickel is like $1.80. The counterman gave
me a piece, about three inches big. I just chomped
away. It's like Jewish tobacco.

Pets: Two dogs in another house I own in Woodland Hills.

Bad Habits: Overzealous cleanliness.

Greatest Achievement: My son and his bar mitzvah.

Biggest Mistake: Turning down *The Music Man*.

Hero: Franklin Delano Roosevelt.

Vacation Spot: Antibes.

Close Friend: Morey Amsterdam, my mentor when I was
starting out, who helped me write an act when I
opened at Loews State.

Home: Beverly Hills.

*I don't speak Yiddish
but I understand it.
My parents spoke Yiddish
if they wanted to say something
without my knowing,
but I picked it up.*

Carol Connors

Her real name is Annette Kleinbard, a super songwriter
who gave the world "Gonna Fly Now," which became the
theme song of Sylvester Stallone's movie *Rocky*; "With
You I'm Born Again;" "To Know Him Is to Love Him;" and
"To Face the World Alone," theme song of *Sophie's Choice*.

"One of the reasons I changed my name," she says, "is I
got tired of saying 'Let me spell it for you.' I always loved
Connors, and I thought Carol went nicely with it. I'm in
good company with Carroll O'Connor, Mike Connor,
Chuck Connors, Jimmy Connors—we have a built-in
family.

"There is even a porno queen named Carol L. Connors.
She was a nurse in *Deep Throat*. I met her at a party at
Hugh Hefner's mansion in Beverly Hills and asked what
the L stands for, 'Left out?' She said no, it stands for
'Luscious.' I said, give me a break."

Carol is very close to her family. She did not make her
chic name change legal. When she bought her house in
Beverly Hills, the name on the papers read Annette
Kleinbard.

"My mother doesn't want me to change my name legally. It would hurt her a lot, for some reason. I love my
parents very much. It's not that important for me to
change it."

Profile

Carol Connors

Given Name: Annette Kleinbard.
Birthday: November 13, 1940.
Birthplace: New Brunswick, New Jersey.
Parents: Gail and Julius Kleinbard.
Height: 4' 11".
Weight: 96 lbs.
Eyes: Green-gray.
Hair: Black.
Zodiac: Scorpio.
Education: One and a half years of anthropology on scholarship at UCLA.
Marriages: None.
Children: None.
Interests: Horseback riding, water skiing.
Personal Habits: Chocolate.
Politics: Democrat.
Jewish Identity: Attends synagogue on High Holidays.
Home: Beverly Hills.

At the Academy Awards, where she was nominated a second time (for writing the theme song of the Walt Disney movie *The Rescuers*), Fred Astaire read the nominations: "Carol O'Connor...Carol Connors...."

"Annettele," her father said, "if you used your own name, Fred Astaire would not have tripped."

"Daddy," Carol replied, "if I had have used my own name, Fred Astaire would not have pronounced it."

Her father Julius was so excited about going to the Oscars that he went out and bought himself a tuxedo. He never had one in his life.

"To take a date is fine," Carol says, "but who would want to see you most at the Academy Awards? Your parents, right? Why not take them? A limo holds four people."

Before she became successful, Carol had to endure the age-old parental harangue: "When are you going to get married and have children?"

Her father was so short, he became a jockey in New York, Pimlico and Cuba. "He's a renegade," she laughs. "Probably the only Jewish jockey in the world."

Julius would say, "If only you could have been a boy, you could have been a jockey."

Now her parents go around and say, "I'm Carol Connors' father." "I'm Carol Connors' mother."

"It gives me as much *naches* (joy) as it gives them," Carol admits.

Although she doesn't keep kosher, she doesn't mix milk with meat. "The thought makes me nauseous."

Like her dad, Carol is petite. She was an incubator baby, a mere four pounds at birth.

"My mother found out her family was annihilated at Auschwitz. She was devastated. It got to the point where she was crying so much she could have died. I was born prematurely, out of this pain my mother was going through for her family.

"Mother said I saved her life. When she saw me, her life was reborn. 'You gave me life and courage because I knew I had to take care of you,' she said."

*The important thing is
to be fortified enough not to let
the world step all over you.
Making sure you have enough
money stored away for you
somewhere, having security
—that's very Jewish.*

David Copperfield

Certainly, Hy Kotkin the clothier never dreamed his little David would actually make a career from a dummy. David would watch ventriloquist Paul Winchell cavort with his wooden sidekick, Jerry Mahoney, on television, and become enthralled with the art of throwing your voice. He studied the act on the small screen devotedly, read some books on theory and nudged his dad to buy him a dummy. His father relented, in the mistaken belief that it was only an early avocation.

See how TV can influence a child's life goal? David immediately made that hobby pay off. At age ten, he entertained at birthday parties in his native Metuchen, New Jersey. They paid him five dollars for a few magic tricks, a little ventriloquism, and blowing up animal balloons.

Soon he asked for seven dollars and fifty cents, and got it. Then he escalated to thirty-five dollars. Unbeknownst to his father, who was busy running Korby's Men's Store in nearby Warren, David's career was taking on momentum.

Hyman and Rebecca Kotkin were typical Jewish parents, in that they wanted their son to grow up to be a doctor, lawyer, or at least in business. "Very standard Jewish ritual there," David says.

We were sitting in the conference room of his public relations representative, Solters Roskin Friedman, on Wilshire Boulevard in Los Angeles. The second conference room was occupied by partners Lee Solters and Monroe Friedman, plotting publicity strategy for such clients as Barbra Streisand and Frank Sinatra. (Sheldon Roskin helms the original office in Manhattan, where I toiled as a publicist during the last New York World's Fair.)

"My parents encouraged me in ventriloquism," David went on. "They felt it would help improve my poise. When I started to take an enormous interest in it as a career, they really tried to steer me away, as any Jewish parent would. They'd say, 'Don't do that, we don't want you starving in the street.' The harder they pushed in the other direction, the harder I tried to prove to myself that I can do it."

The Kotkins belonged to the Nevei Shalom Synagogue and gave David a typical Jewish upbringing, sending him to Hebrew school every day. Hyman was born in Brooklyn. His parents came from Russia. Rebecca is a sabra, having been born in Jerusalem. She came to the United States when she was five years old.

After high school, David enrolled at Fordham University in Manhattan. He was there only three weeks when he was hired for *The Magic Man*, a musical comedy in Chicago. The advertisement in *Variety* sought an actor-magician. He was a magician, and now he became an actor overnight.

He progressed swiftly, doing his amazing illusions on his own annual television show on CBS. One year he made a jumbo plane disappear; the next year he made the Statue of

Liberty vanish. It was all done in front of hundreds of witnesses, so the television home audience knows there is no fancy camera editing involved. His latest feat was walking through the Great Wall of China.,

His most satisfying achievement is Project Magic, which he started four years ago. He would get letters from aspiring young magicians asking for advice. One letter included an article about a young magician in a wheel chair. This person had written before but did not mention that he was in a wheel chair. He advertises in the phone book, never mentioning that he is handicapped. The newspaper reporter had asked what happens when the audience reacts to the fact that he is disabled. The young magician replied, that is their problem. He does not perceive himself as being disabled. He thinks of himself as someone special, doing magic.

"I thought back to my childhood," says David. "I didn't have very many friends. Magic really helped me get friends and feel special instead of different. I decided that giving the gift of magic can really help someone get their self-esteem as well as help their physical skills.

"By learning sleight of hand, you could regain your dexterity and coordination. You'd be motivated by doing magic. In addition to boosting the patient's self-esteem by giving him a skill, magic, he is able to do something that an able-bodied person does not even have. So he can feel better than, as opposed to feeling less than."

That is the idea of Project Magic. David recruited other magicians to visit five hundred hospitals in thirty countries around the world. There are, today, thousands of magicians helping patients emotionally and physically. Mr. Kotkin, your David became a doctor after all. It just took a little magic.

David is so devoted to his art that his next ambition is to sway society's attitude to a more positive view of magic. He would like to see magic perceived on the same level as dance, music and theater.

That's why he is irked by illusionists who pass themselves off as endowed with psychic powers, when all they do is magic. David once confronted the famed Israeli spoon-bender Uri Geller on the Irv Kupcinet television program in Chicago. Each time Geller bent a spoon, Copperfield did the same thing.

"Being a magician," David avers, "you know how everything works. You become a skeptic about mystical things. I've never seen anybody bend keys or spoons or do anything supernatural.

"Uri is a magician. He calls himself a psychic. The people who are going out and making a name for themselves are not doing it by psychic powers. They are doing it with physical techniques.

"Uri Geller? He is a good magician. That's it. He bent a spoon. So did I."

David says he has stopped going after such people to disprove their claims and show that they are really magicians. Such magicians will still have their audiences believing them to be what they claim to be, psychics, because people want to believe in the supernatural.

"However," says David, "I don't want to see somebody stop using medication because some psychic person tells him to stop, when there is a medical problem that needs to be attended to physically."

Profile
David Copperfield

Given Name: David Kotkin.
Birthday: September 16, 1956.
Birthplace: Metuchen, N.J.
Parents: Hyman Kotkin and Rebecca Gispan
Siblings: None.
Height: 6'
Weight: 140 lbs.
Eyes: Brown.
Hair: Brown.
Zodiac: Virgo.
Education: Metuchen High School.
Marriages: None.
Interests: Films.
Lifestyle: I live on the road, travel a lot.
Personal Habits: Don't smoke, drink or gamble. My crew won't let me play poker with them—unfair advantage.
Clubs: None.
Politics: Nonpartisan.
Social Life: Dancing, going out.
First Job: I always did magic, since age 10 at birthday parties. I wish I had a job at McDonald's, more life experience.
Favorite Movies: *Wizard of Oz, Gone With The Wind, Citizen Kane, Harold and Maude.*
Snack: Fresh fruit.

Car: Cadillac Seville; use Ferrari in my act—but I don't drive, don't have a license.

Pets: Webster the duck whom I use in my act.

Exercise: Just doing the show is exercise.

Charity: Project Magic.

Ambition: Filmmaking.

Biggest Mistake: Allowing myself to believe that a stressful life means success. I didn't enjoy success more. I wasted a lot of time when I should have been relaxing.

Biggest Irritant: A year ago I could have given you a ton of things. Now I don't let things bother me. I laugh them off.

Hero: Walt Disney, Orson Welles. I love fantasy.

Bad Habits: Eating meat.

Greatest Achievement: Making the Statue of Liberty disappear. Project Magic will live on to help people after I die.

Vacation Spot: Hawaii.

Kosher: No.

Synagogue: None.

Observe Holidays: In my own way. Occasionally I'd go to my relatives for the seder.

Jewish Identity: To do as much good for society while you are here.

Home: Los Angeles; Las Vegas.

I'm Jewish but play WASP parts;
I'm a singer but don't sing much.
I'm turning down scripts. I got one
script for an "exquisite beauty,"
and wondered why I got it. I read
on. There were forty pages of
nudity. I turned it down.
Quoted by Earl Wilson
New York Post
July 9, 1980

TOVAH FELDSHUH

One script Tovah Feldshuh did not rebuff was the title role of Isaac Bashevis Singer's *Yentl* on Broadway in 1975. This is the extraordinary tale of a shtetl girl who yearned to study the Talmud so much that she disguised herself as a boy in order to be accepted in a yeshiva. Although she was raised in a Jewishly conscious home in high-toned Scarsdale, and had a good Hebrew education, she felt she had to brush up for the role. So she studied with a rebbe in Borough Park, a section of Brooklyn populated by Orthodox Jews.

After her play opened on Broadway, these same Orthodox fans were outraged by a scene where Yentl the yeshiva boy opens his shirt to reveal that he is actually a woman. Public protests forced the play to close.

One morning, Tovah dons her skintight riding shorts and biker's helmet and maneuvers her bicycle from her Upper West Side apartment to meet me at the Stage Deli. The first thing I want to know is the derivation of her intriguing name.

Tovah, of course, is Hebrew for "good." Feldshuh, pronounced "fellshoe," means "field boot" in German. Her birth certificate records her as Terri Sue Feldshuh, named after her Aunt Matilda (Tovah) and her mother's Grandma Sarah. She says Tovah also means "tree of Paradise" in Arabic, "dove" in Danish and "comrade" in Russian.

"There were two boys at Scarsdale High who were named Terry," Tovah says. "My godfather's dog was Terry. Enough of this. Tovah is much more romantic and very emotional, which I am."

Terri always sounded foreign, strange. She wanted a woman's name. So everybody began calling her Tovah. At seventeen, when she entered Sarah Lawrence College, she took Tovah legally.

When I met her five years ago for lunch at Moshe Peking, the elegant kosher Chinese restaurant in Manhattan, she acknowledged that Tovah always brought her great luck. Now she is not quite sure. She feels she made a mistake in not changing this very special ethnic sounding name to something more homogeneous, a middle-of-the-road appellation such as Terry Fairchild. She can play all types of characters, but her ethnic-sounding name marks her as a serious type and brings her roles in Chekhov, Shakespeare and other classics. She is always called to play ethnic roles—Italians, Jews, Irish.

On television she electrified a world with her skillful portrayal of Helena Slomova, a Czech freedom fighter, in *Holocaust* (1978). On Broadway, besides Yentl the yeshiva boy (1975), she played a sensual Brazilian woman in *Sarava* (1979). Her name clinched a role as Miriam Polodnik, Sam Levene's daughter, in *Dreyfus in Rehearsal* (1974). This marked her dramatic debut in an ingenue part. Garson Kanin, the director, said with a name like Tovah

Feldshuh, she must be right for the role of a Jewish girl in 1931 Poland. In her screen debut, she played an Irish Catholic editor of a teen magazine in *The Idol Maker* (1980).

Apparently, she presents a case when she maintains that producers tend to typecast her in ethnic roles because of her name. "I've trained myself for all sorts of roles and my name seems to limit me," she notes.

Had she stayed with her earliest ambition, she would not have found herself in this professional dilemma. Her father is a Harvard-trained lawyer and Tovah wanted to follow in his footsteps. She applied to Harvard Law School and was put on the waiting list. Meantime, she won a McKnight Fellowship at the Tyrone Guthrie Theater in Minneapolis. Her brother, David Feldshuh, is a physician in that city and a director at the theater. Tovah gave up a law career to spend two seasons at the Guthrie, which proved to be of inestimable value in preparation for the acting life.

In a sense, her original dream has also been realized. In 1977, she married Andrew Harris Levy, a Harvard lawyer who is active with the American Jewish Committee. Now there are two attorneys in the family. There may yet be a third. She gave birth to a son, Garson Brandon Levy.

"I married a brilliant lawyer," she kvells. "I do not regret giving up law school at Harvard. He completes that part of my life for me."

Tovah's father is Sidney Feldshuh, a financial consultant and attorney. Her mother Lillian is a past vice president of the American Jewish Congress. They live in Westchester and are members of Temple Israel in White Plains.

The actress is very involved with helping Jewish causes, such as freeing Soviet Jews. She is an engrossing speaker at fund-raising events for the United Jewish Appeal.

"I am very happy to be who I am," she affirms. "Having kept this name has harnessed me for Jewish affairs and I am grateful for that. All the Jewish charities mean a great deal to me. They are in the business of making lives work."

Profile
Tovah Feldshuh

Given Name: Terri Sue Feldshuh.
Birthday: December 27, 1953.
Birthplace: New York City.
Parents: Lillian and Sidney Feldshuh.
Siblings: Brother, Dr. David Feldshuh.
Height: 5′3″.
Weight: 105 lbs.
Eyes: Hazel.
Hair: Brown.
Zodiac: Capricorn.
Education: Scarsdale High School; Sarah Lawrence College.
Marriage: Andrew Harris Levy (1977).
Children: Garson Brandon (b. 1983).
Interests: Exercise.
Lifestyle: Adventuresome; ski in French Alps.
Clubs: Harvard Club; Writers and Artists for Peace in the Middle East.
Politics: Democrat.
Social Life: Unrelenting social life; go out a lot; go to theater.
Pets: None. I love cats, but my husband is allergic to them.
Ambition: To be in Theater Hall of Fame; to do a TV series.
Charities: UJA; abortion rights.

Biggest mistake: Not changing my name to Fairchild.

Biggest Irritant: 1) When people ask me if I wasn't in *Fiddler on the Roof.* I was in grade school at the time. 2) When people mistakenly think I'm this Hebrew-speaking or Yiddish-speaking foreigner. 3) When people grab my cheeks.

Hero: Eleanor Roosevelt.

Bad Habits: Pick my cuticles; sweet tooth.

Greatest Achievement: 1) Winning Eleanor Roosevelt Humanitarian Award from UJA for my work for Israel. 2) Bringing my son into the world.

Kosher: No.

Observe Holidays: Yom Kippur, Passover.

Favorite Book: *Zen and Art of Archery.*

Favorite Movie: *The Ten Commandments.*

Favorite TV Show: *60 Minutes.*

Snack: Frozen fruit.

Car: Mercedes.

First Job: Tutoring Spanish and French during high school.

Career Start: Leading ingenue in summer stock 1969 at Theater by the Sea, Matunuck, R.I.

Vacation Spot: South of France; skiing in French Alps.

Home: Manhattan.

Teenage superstar Eddie Fisher before he discovered wine and women — but not before song.

*I couldn't help
being attracted to beautiful
women, almost always women
who were not Jewish, because they
were forbidden. And I was excited
when they responded to me,
whatever their motives. Going out
with a pretty shiksa, going to bed
with her, was like spending a lot of
money—a way of proving I was
no longer a poor Jew from the
slums of Philadelphia.
I was somebody.*

Eddie: My Life, My Loves

EDDIE FISHER

As he says, the only sexual advice he received from his parents was to stay away from non-Jewish girls. Who listens to parents? The only women who attracted him were shiksas. They quickly became his paramours. He bedded such personalities as Mamie Van Doren, Maria Schell, Stephanie Powers, Judy Garland, Edie Adams, Merle Oberon, Ann-Margret, Terry Moore and Mia Farrow.

Of the four beauties he did marry—Debbie Reynolds, Elizabeth Taylor, Connie Stevens, Terry Richard—only one converted to his faith. Elizabeth became a Jew before she married him.

"She sincerely believed in what she had done," Eddie says of the Reform conversion Elizabeth went through, with Rabbi Max Nussbaum of Temple Israel, in Los Angeles. "Then she forgot all about it. We didn't go to synagogue. We celebrated Yom Kippur only once."

Since his broken marriages, Eddie continues to seek

solace, and look for love, with non-Jewish companions. When I visited him at his cozy West Side apartment in Manhattan, his live-in love was a tall, gorgeous blond from California, a psychotherapist named Lindsay Davis.

Is he ready for a fifth attempt at matrimonial bliss?

"All I can say," he replied, "is that looking back on my life, and on my patterns, I think there is a great possibility that I'll make another mistake."

We both laughed.

His pattern, as you can see, has been a course of inter-marriage. I was curious about that. Here is a famous personality who stems from a distinctly Jewish background, whose signature songs have been the very moving *Oh, My Papa* and *My Yiddishe Mama*, that drain tears from sensitive listeners—and he chooses a non-Jewish partner each time he takes that walk up the aisle.

"We'll have to talk to a psychologist about that," was his answer. "Haven't many Jewish boys strayed from the fold who have married shiksas?"

"Not with the consistency you have shown," I told him. "Can't you find a nice Jewish girl, Eddie?"

"I think it is too late for me. For what I have been through and what I have found, it is too late for me to find a nice Jewish girl in show business. The woman I have now is not Jewish, but she is a very spiritual woman, very religious in her thinking. As a matter of fact, she has changed a lot of my thinking. Not as far as being a Jew. I am a Jew, first and always. Proud that I am a Jew. That is my *shtoltz.*"

I ask how he expresses his Jewishness.

"I have a deep concern for Israel. I am a Zionist. I believe in America; I believe in Israel."

For Jewish audiences, Eddie offers a treasure of Yiddish and Hebrew melodies.

"The Yiddish songs were taught me by my mother when I was very young. We were very poor then. She bought me a second-hand upright piano for fifteen dollars which she could not afford. And she would buy the sheet music. She could read the right hand, and that's why I can only read the right hand.

"I was singing before I was walking. My first professional job was in the temple, where I made twenty dollars for the High Holidays. I was the soloist with the tall white *yarmulke.* I must have been ten."

Success followed swiftly, as he segued from cantor to crooner. At thirteen he won a *Children's Hour* radio contest. While playing at Grossinger's in 1949, the Borscht Belt vocalist was discovered by comedian Eddie Cantor, who took him on a cross-country tour—and the rest is history. His meteoric rise to the heights of stardom was littered with failed marriages, fleeting sexual affairs, drug addictions, gambling forays, debts and bankruptcy—and he eventually plummeted off the fast track.

Through it all, he was sustained by the love and support of his children, if not his ex-wives. His son Todd, by Debbie Reynolds, took him into his Los Angeles house, and helped his father get himself together when he hit rock bottom. Later his daughter Carrie, also by Debbie, took him into her New York apartment for a year.

"Carrie has played a major role in my turnaround. She made me come to New York. That was my beginning. A new beginning. A renewed Jew."

The kids were a great source of comfort when he was feeling his worst. That is surprising, considering that he was not particularly close to his children when they were growing up.

After Debbie divorced Eddie, she took custody of the children. When she married Jewish shoe tycoon Harry Karl, she promised Eddie she would raise Todd in the Jewish faith.

In his autobiography, Eddie recounts in poignant prose the time he visited them at their home in Malibu. Carrie was four; Todd was two. He asked their mother if she still intended to bring Todd up as a Jew, and she told him, "I changed my mind."

An astonished Eddie muttered, "Debbie, I didn't ask you to do it. You brought the subject up yourself. It was your idea and you made a promise."

"Well," she said, "I was in love with you then. I'm not in love with you now."

Then Harry added: "We have nothing against the Jews. But we go to a very nice Methodist church with a very fine minister. If he had ever said anything against the Jews, would I have given him $7,500?"

Eddie told me he left their house "full of anger and resentment."

Todd today is married to Donna Freberg, daughter of comedy writer Stan Freberg, who is not Jewish. Close friend Debby Boone had introduced Donna to Bible study. Subsequently, Todd became a born-again Christian, too. He was ordained, and helped found the Hiding Place Church in Westwood.

A weekly tabloid reported that Todd had converted his father.

"It wasn't true, of course," Eddie avowed.

Nevertheless, that erroneous story sent shock waves through the placid Catskill mountains, source of Eddie's early triumphs. Grossinger's, which had been his second home, did not take his calls and refused to book him. When the Concord welcomed him, after he disavowed the story, Grossinger's then relented.

I asked where he stood in his beliefs. He admitted that his son "did try to influence me," but stated emphatically that he was not moved.

"I have always been a Jew," he declares. "I am proud to be a Jew. I am Anschel Yankel Fisher."

Eddie with Lindsay Davis.

Eddie Fisher

Given Name: Edwin Jack Fisher.
Birthday: August 10, 1928.
Birthplace: Philadelphia.
Parents: Joseph Fisher and Katherine Minicker.
Siblings: Six.
Zodiac: Leo.
Marriages: 1. Debbie Reynolds (1955-59); 2. Elizabeth Taylor (1959-64); 3. Connie Stevens (1968-69); 4. Terry Richard (1975-76).
Children: 1. Carrie Francis (b. 1956) by Debbie Reynolds;   2. Todd Emmanuel (b. 1958) by Debbie Reynolds;   3. Joely (b. 1967) by Connie Stevens; 4. Trisha Leigh   (b. 1968) by Connie Stevens.

NBC's THE GOLDEN GIRLS: *Estelle Getty* (**front center**), *with* (**left to right**) *Bea Arthur, Rue McClanahan and Betty White.*

*I never underestimate
the importance of the playwright.
That's why I've learned never to
take credit for anything. I've
appeared in many obscure and
strange plays, some good, some
bad. But when I had the mother
role, no matter what the reviews, I
always got good notices. People
thought it was a tribute to my
talent, but it was the only good
writing in the play. The one
truthful character, no matter what
the drama, is always the mother.
Everyone has had one.*
Quoted by Kay Gardella
New York Daily News

Estelle Getty

She is everyone's idea of *mamaleh*, the archetypal, universal, quintessential Jewish mother. She played Cher's mother in the film *Mask*, and Barry Manilow's mother in the television movie *Copacabana*. She played an Irish mother, an Italian mother, a Midwestern mother. In fifty-five years of acting, she has played everybody's mother, everybody but Attila the Hun.

She scored overnight success on Broadway when she played Harvey Fierstein's Jewish mother, in his Tony Award winning show *Torch Song Trilogy.*

On television, she has triumphed as the yente mama of one of the three mature women in NBC's highly rated situation comedy *The Golden Girls.* Only in her early sixties, she deftly portrays the eighty-year-old mother of sixty-three-year-old Bea Arthur.

At a press conference arranged by the network at the Century Plaza Hotel, Estelle was asked how she made herself look that old.

"Not with makeup," she replied. "It's done with acting."

"Oh, come on," Bea interjected. "What's that acting you sprayed on your hair?"

The four cast members proved to be as bright and funny in person as they are in the show. Each actress—Bea, the gray haired one; Estelle, the redhead; Rue McLanahan, the brunette; Betty White, the blond—has a sharp sense of humor. On the show, this is enhanced by excellent writing that is full of wit and fun.

Now, tell the truth. When you think of four ladies sharing their golden years under one roof in Miami, do you not think at least one would be Jewish? I mean, this is Miami, the Cuban influx notwithstanding.

The show's debut raised eyebrows when Estelle was introduced as the feisty, outspoken yente Sophia Petrillo, octogenarian mother of Dorothy (played by Bea Arthur, the Jewish actress who was the liberal yente in *Maude*).

Even Estelle found it odd that there was no Jewish character in this Miami setting. It would have been a lot easier to play the role if the grandma were Jewish, but writer-creator Susan Harris wrote it as Italian.

"That's very strange to me," Estelle says, "and it was one of my objections. I could not understand why they could not have made me Jewish. The writer wanted Italian. I asked her, if there are three women living together, one of them surely could be Jewish. She said no.

"The writer is Jewish, but she says she wrote the role for an Italian mother and daughter. Of the other two, one is a WASP from the South (Rue McLanahan's Blanche), and the other Episcopalian (Betty White's Rose), I guess. I don't know. We keep religion out of it, except for me. I keep saying I'm Catholic all the time. It doesn't really affect me. I've played many roles in my life, some of them very distasteful, some of them wonderful. I like this role and that's what I play. That's my job. That's what I do. I don't write them, I act them."

She has been acting them since she was a child of four, and lived at 55 Pitt Street on the Lower East Side. Up the block lived a man who sang in the Yiddish theater. They needed a little girl for a play, so they took Estelle. They put her in a cage with a long pole across the middle on which she would sit and swing. That was the start of a career on the Yiddish stage.

Her parents were enthusiastic fans of the Yiddish theater. Charles and Sarah Scher came from small towns in Galicia, in Austria-Poland. He was a glazier who operated an auto glass shop on the street where they lived. They belonged to a *farein*, an immigrant social group, that would always buy tickets to the Yiddish plays. Estelle was exposed to show business at an early age. She was sent to the Educational Alliance to study dancing, acting and singing.

"My parents were in business around the clock, six days a week," she recalls. "It was very hard for them. But someone would always take me to the classes. My sister, who is three years older, used to take me. I managed, somehow, because everything was within walking distance."

Estelle was given a minimal Hebrew education. She describes her sister as the smarter one, who attended Downtown Talmud Torah, and consequently can read Hebrew and *daven* (pray with a *siddur*). Estelle had a *melamed* (Hebrew teacher) named Lipa Keller.

"My head was always somewhere else. He used to stick me with his pointed stick."

He came to the house for the lessons; everybody came to the house. The family lived in back of the shop. Charles Scher was the central point in everyone's life. Everybody came to converse with him. He was a raconteur and very funny. The kitchen was usually full of people and conversation.

Around the corner was the Nine 'n' Ninetziker Shul, a little synagogue at 99 Houston Street. Estelle's father would go there often, because he loved the philosophical debates. He was not that religious, but he was a scholar.

Her father used to take Estelle to see the movie and vaudeville at the Academy of Music on Fourteenth Street. The live acts made a lasting impression on her. She knew instinctively that her destination lay beyond the boundaries of the Lower East Side.

"I always wondered what life was like above Fourteenth Street and Klein's Department Store," she says. "I didn't know what it was, but I knew there was something out there for me that wasn't for everybody else. I guess I was a very neurotic child. While other kids were playing jacks, jumping rope and playing ball, I was at the Educational Alliance and the Grand Street Settlement, taking acting lessons. That is where I knew I belonged."

After high school, Estelle worked in offices during the day and worked as an actress at night and on weekends.

"My father never believed I'd be an actress. He thought sooner or later the meshigas would go away."

It never did, of course. Estelle became a familiar figure off-off-Broadway. She met Fierstein at La Mama Experimental Theater in the East Village, where he performed one of his plays. Subsequently, she nudged him to write in a part for a Jewish mother, which he did in *Torch Song Trilogy*.

Now Estelle spends a good part of the year shooting *The Golden Girls* at the Sunset-Gower Studios in Los Angeles. Her husband joins her every few weeks. He is Arthur Gettleman who, after marrying Estelle, went into her dad's business and became a glazier. Today he runs a glass business in Port Washington, Long Island. Home is an apartment in Bayside, Queens. They have two sons: Carl, a writer, named for Estelle's father, and Barry, a budget director with the Metropolitan Transit Authority of New York City.

She was Estelle Scher until she married. The name did not necessarily denote Jewishness. So she did not have trouble getting a job during the Depression, when other individuals named Rosenberg or Greenblatt were flatly turned away.

"Many companies didn't hire Jews," she says. "I was glad my name was Scher. It was in my favor. In a way, I suppose, I passed. But I can tell you that I never have, and never will, do that again. If six million people had to die for it, I sure as hell am not going to contribute to it."

For two decades she was billed as Estelle Gettleman. It proved to be a hard name for producers and agents to remember. They called her Gentleman much of the time.

"At one point, about fifteen years ago, I decided to change. It took me a very long time to make that decision. I wanted to make sure I was doing it for the right reason, not so I would simply Anglo-Saxonize it. I found out it was a very difficult name to get by on. The name was hard to say and hard to read. So I shortened it to Getty."

Estelle had always taken her name and heritage seriously. She speaks Yiddish fluently. She kept kosher in Queens, so her Orthodox mother could eat in her home. She sent her two boys to a Conservative Hebrew school, and they still observe the High Holidays like their mother and father. The parents belong to the Oakland Jewish Center and Young Israel in Bayside.

While she may work on such holidays as Passover, Shavuot and Sukkot, Estelle refrains from working on Rosh Hashanah and Yom Kippur, the most solemn days of the Jewish calendar.

"In the theater, it's easier to do that than in television and movies. In the theater, your understudy goes on for you. In television and movies, there is no one to go on for you. So far I've been lucky and able to do it."

It is very hard to observe the Jewish religious holidays in show business. Estelle tries. In the spring of 1986, she was filming in Philadelphia during Passover. Her stand-in invited her to her home for the seder. Estelle's husband came from New York to join them.

Sam Levenson, the late great Jewish humorist, impressed Estelle tremendously when he told her to never, ever, deny that you're Jewish. If someone is talking about Jews, never pretend that you are not one. And never let an anti-Semitic remark go by, thinking that the individual is only ignorant. Because that is how it all starts. You must address every anti-Semitic remark, and that includes those coming from Jews.

On Orchard Street, the bustling bargain boulevard of the Lower East Side, Estelle saw a woman *handlen* (bargaining). One man said to his partner, *"Nor a Yid vet dos getun"* (Only a Jew would do this).

"Why do you say that?" Estelle demanded. "We have enough enemies."

"It's all right," the man replied. "I can say that, I am Jewish."

"It's not all right," Estelle shot back. "We have enough people saying that. We don't need Jews saying that about other Jews."

Such incidents are painful to Estelle. "There is nothing sadder or more bitter than an anti-Semitic Jew." She cannot tolerate Jews who are afraid to admit they are Jews, or who are reluctant to talk about it.

"That hurts me terribly. They would be the first ones to weep for the six million Jews. Yet they will never address the issue themselves. I can't imagine why. I don't know what makes people think that way. But it has always been very painful to me when a person says, 'I don't want to talk about my Jewishness.' I don't think you will ever hear a Catholic say, 'I don't want to talk about being Catholic.' Even if they don't follow the religion, they will talk about it."

Estelle got a bonus when *Lifestyles of the Rich and Famous* tapped her for a profile. They wanted to film her in Los Angeles, but her roommate was moving, and there were boxes all over the apartment on Sunset Boulevard. Her Queens apartment was out of the question, because it was so small, not something you would feature on a television program with such a glamorous title.

She ended up doing it in Israel. She had not been there since a family vacation fifteen years ago. It was a real treat. She found few tourists in the land, due to the terrorist problem. So she boldly made a pitch on the television program, saying it was, indeed, safe to visit Israel. The Minister of Tourism, of course, was delighted with her forthrightness.

The Israelis were not familiar with her name, as *The Golden Girls* is not on television there yet. No matter, Estelle says, the Israelis do not have much time for television.

She was amazed how Americanized they have become, what with discos and bars.

"It was still very exciting. The people are still gung ho for their country. It's very nice to go there. What a feeling to see the policemen are Jews. It's a total Jewish environment. There's a sense of safety you feel, everybody being your own people. You stand there and watch a garbage truck go by, a police car, a cement mixer. It was a wonderful experience."

Profile
Estelle Getty

Given Name: Estelle Scher
Birthday: July 25, 1924.
Birthplace: New York City.
Parents: Charles and Sarah Scher.
Siblings: Sister, bookkeeper; and brother, court stenographer.
Height: 5' (I never tell anybody my height; I'm too small.)
Weight: 103 lbs.
Eyes: Blue.
Hair: Dyed reddish-brown.
Zodiac: Leo.
Education: Took many courses at New School for Social Research but never matriculated.
Marriage: Arthur Gettleman, for 38 years.
Children: Two sons: Carl, writer; and Barry, budget director.
Personal Habits: Smoke occasionally; enjoy wine.
Clubs: Connected with every major Jewish organization at various times: B'nai B'rith, Hadassah, ORT, National Council of Jewish Women; also, League of Women Voters.
Politics: Little to the left of Democrat.
Social Life: I'm a very social creature; I go out a lot with many friends whom I see all the time.

First Job: At 14, I worked at a second-hand clothing exporter.

Favorite Book: Herman Wouk's *Marjorie Morningstar,* which I thought was the story of my life.

Snack: Sweets, candy, cookies.

Car: Toyota Tercel in Hollywood; Mercedes-Benz in Queens.

Pets: No more since the cat took off.

Ambition: I've done everything I've wanted to do: plays, television, movies. Everything is going very well for me. Not to be a *chazer* (pig), one must know when to say God's been good and be grateful for that.

Exercise: Exercycle, walking, stretching.

Charity: I contribute to every appeal, especially National Jewish Home for Children in Denver, because my son was an asthmatic.

Biggest Mistake: Not matriculating in college. I'm so envious of people with a degree.

Biggest Irritant: Excessively shy people who don't contribute. Also gratuitous cruelty, people who are not aware of other people's feelings.

Hero: Anybody who devotes his life to medicine, science, or helping others.

Home: Queens, N.Y.

I call myself unorthodox.
But the greater part of unorthodox
is orthodox.

ELLIOTT GOULD

For two weeks I had been calling Elliott Gould at his home in Brentwood, California, but he was busy preparing for the premiere of his second television series, *Together We Stand*, on CBS. I caught up with him at a Chabad residence for drug abuse treatment. He had brought Whoopi Goldberg to meet the dozen male residents who, after years of being spaced out in the L.A. drug scene, were cleaning up their act with the help of social workers at this Lubavitch Hasidim center. There were Jews and Gentiles, whites and blacks, being guided off the high flying drug merry-go-round.

Elliott was still too busy to see me. He and Whoopi had been invited by Chabad leader Rabbi Shlomo Cunin to make a videotape of their visit to the rehabilitating druggies to be shown on the Chabad fall telethon. Jerry Cutler, rabbi at the Sholom Aleichem Temple of the Creative Arts, produces the annual telethon, for which the leading Hollywood locals cancel lunch at the Friars or the Polo Lounge to help the Hasidim raise funds for their Outreach programs.

Two days before I was to return to the East Coast, Elliott came to my room at the Beverly Hilton and, for an hour, talked profoundly about his religious convictions, his beliefs about himself and his family, his outlook on life and how he grew up. Although he is not religious in the traditional observant manner, he is aware of certain forces in life influencing him, and strives to learn as much as he can about the reality that exists around him.

"I try to keep kosher in my mind now," he says. "That's working out. That really appeals to me. Mental kosher and spiritual kosher. As for physical kosher, like I say, I'm learning to respect it. I've been in kosher homes and it's a great idea."

But apparently he is not ready to try it yet. It will take some doing for him to spring from respect to acceptance. Perhaps that's because he has been removed from Jewish customs since coming of age at thirteen. He practiced and studied and rehearsed for his bar mitzvah. All his education was aimed at making a bar mitzvah boy out of him. After it was over, his Jewish education was over. He hadn't learned a thing.

Elliott Goldstein was born in Far Rockaway, Queens, in 1939, and a year later moved to 6801 Bay Parkway, in Bensonhurst, Brooklyn. After attending PS 247, he would go to late afternoon classes at an Orthodox Hebrew school. His father Bernard, a Brooklyn native, toiled in the textile business as a buyer and production manager. His mother Lucille, born in Manhattan, operated a millinery shop in Brooklyn. Elliott's grandparents came from Russia and Poland.

All the values Elliott holds dear he inherited from his parents. He remembers when his mother and grandmother would light the Shabbat candles on Friday nights. Now and then, he attends a Seder with friends on Passover. "My friends, the Hasidim, who are really observant, let me know what's happening, so I'm becoming more and more aware," he says.

A favorite holiday is the eight-day observance of Chanukah, when he loves to light the menorah, commemorating the Jewish victory over Greek-Syrian forces attempting to stifle religious freedom in ancient Israel. People give presents, customarily coins, to the children. One year, on the last day of the holiday, when all eight candles were burning, plus the extra one called the *shammes*, Elliott told his two children, "Tonight, instead of money, I'm going to give you total honesty and truth, which is more important." Of course that did not fool little Molly, who remarked, "But you give us that every night."

So he is just now catching up, with the help of his friends at Chabad, on a Jewish education he never really grasped as a kid.

"I couldn't understand, and I didn't really want to understand, why and how people could practice Orthodox, but live with double values and live with another face, not really actualize the purpose of the religion in relation with my ideal for life. I became aware of it at a very early age, and I think it may have traumatized me a little bit."

But he approaches it all with an open mind. Relating one's spiritual values to reality is of paramount importance to him. "What is reality? I believe reality is my religion. It's real to me. There are certain aspects to life and death that are also real."

The actor's link to reality is his children. He has a son Jason, born in 1967, when he was married to Barbra Streisand. He has two children by his second wife, Jennifer Bogart. His daughter Molly Safire was born in 1972. His son Sam Bazooka came the next year.

Jason had his bar mitzvah at the Bay Cities Synagogue, a well-known Orthodox congregation in Venice, that was founded by author and film critic Michael Medved. Both mother and son attended the requisite Hebrew classes. The shul is supported financially by such film colony inhabitants as Steven Spielberg, Richard Dreyfuss and Barbra Streisand.

Elliott, always very close to his ex-wife, helped arrange the bar mitzvah celebration and came to the big event with his family. Little Molly, five years younger than Jason, was quite impressed with the ceremony, the first Jewish ritual she had ever experienced. She decided she wants a bat mitzvah. She started studying with the synagogue's rabbi, Ben Lapin, who had originally come from South Africa. The rabbi then recommended a private female tutor, who came to the house and worked with the youngster.

"Molly said she wasn't just interested in learning the holidays," the proud daddy reports. "She wanted to study the law, the Talmud. She said she didn't want a bat mitzvah just because it's supposed to be done. She said she really wants to work at it. So the rabbi says she can take all the time she needs until she feels she's ready; then we'll do it, regardless of how old she'll be."

Molly is still studying. She's a serious young girl. "She's a gifted child," her father says. "She was recognized as a gifted child in the Los Angeles public school. That meant she didn't have to bring home so much homework."

What a relief that must have been for daddy!

She came home from studying with Rabbi Lapin one day, and asked her father what the Neptune Society was. He explained that members of that group cremate the departed and spread the ashes over the sea. Neptune, in Greek mythology, was the god of the ocean. Molly, her eight-year-old brain in full gear, looked straight at her father and declared, "I will never let you be burned. I'll bury you in one piece. And you're not dead until you're forgotten."

"And then she tweaked my nose," Elliott recalled. "I was just so amazed, it took my breath away."

He added, "What she stated was the foundation of the religion. I told the rabbi. He said the amazing thing in working with her is to see the knowledge of all time pass through her beautiful mind."

Molly also used to say such things as, "It doesn't matter how long you live, so long as you know you're living."

She also questioned: Why do we call it Hebrew? Why not Shebrew? Webrew? Seminal thinking for a budding feminist.

To arrive at this contented stage in his life, Elliott had to pay heavy dues in his career. He had an unusual Jewish mother. Instead of urging her only son to become a doctor or a lawyer, she actually set his sights on the theater.

By the time he was ten, Elliott was a member of Charles Lowe's Little Kids, a children's song-and-dance group. He would put on his mother's makeup and do a number in the hour-long show presented at weddings and bar mitzvahs. He remembers once when they were on the same bill with Buck & Bubbles, and Josh White, at the Pythian Temple on New York's West Side. It was at this time, when he was singing and dancing on local television, that his mother shortened his name to Gould.

He was graduated from the Professional Children's School in Manhattan in 1955, and embarked on a theatrical career in earnest. He made his Broadway debut at eighteen in the musical comedy *Rumple.* He came to the attention of legendary Broadway producer David Merrick, who signed him to star on the Great White Way in the hit musical *I Can Get It For You Wholesale,* in 1962. However, he was overshadowed by the electric force of an unknown power named Barbra Streisand. Her explosive rendition of the Miss Marmelstein role earned her a standing ovation every night. In fact, the only recognition the musical got at the Tony Awards was the newcomer's nomination for Best Supporting Actress (though she lost out to Phyllis Newman in *Subways Are For Sleeping*).

If neither Elliott, for his first starring role, nor Barbra, for her overwhelming performance, garnered a Tony Award that year, they found solace in each other's arms, as romance was kindled. They wed the following year. The marriage was doomed almost from the beginning, as her star shot up like a meteor, while his sputtered for lack of fuel.

He continued to perform on Broadway (with Barbara Cook in Jules Feiffer's *Little Murders*, in 1967), and in Hollywood (as Billy Minsky with Jason Robards and Bert Lahr in *The Night They Raided Minsky's*, in 1968). Although he made his screen debut in 1964, in *The Confession*, starring Ginger Rogers and Ray Milland, his movie breakthrough did not come until his third film, *Bob and Carol and Ted and Alice*, in 1969. The role of Ted garnered him an Academy Award nomination.

His success continued in 1970, when he starred in four films: *Getting Straight* with Candice Bergen, *I Love My Wife* with Brenda Vaccaro, *Move*, and, of course, *M*A*S*H*, where his creation of the Trapper John role got him an Academy Award nomination. Subsequently, he was selected by famed Swedish director Ingmar Bergman as the first American actor to star in one of his films, *The Touch*, in 1971. That same year he reprised his *Little Murders* role in the movie version.

Suddenly his career took a dive almost to obscurity. There were bickering and problems on the New York film set of *A Glimpse of Tiger*, and after four horrendous days of attempted filming, the studio abruptly scuttled the project. Elliott's eccentric reputation hung in the balance. Two lean years ensued, when studios were reluctant to take the risk of hiring him, followed by eleven years of making largely B movies and other forgettable work. He co-starred with Bill Cosby in 1981 in a Disney movie, *The Devil and Max Devlin*, which the *Los Angeles Times* reviewed as "Cosby, Gould in Hellzafloppin."

After years of analysis and introspection, and a double attempt at matrimonial happiness with Jennifer, fifteen years his junior (whom he married, divorced and remarried), Elliott is at the brink of greatness once again. He found his forte in television, and hopefully his complete comeback on the big screen is at hand.

He has his priorities well laid out. He gets along with everybody. The drugs he used to dabble in are a thing of the past. He told gossip columnist Marilyn Beck that he us-

Elliott Gould and wife Jennifer Bogart in 1972 in New York.

ed "foreign substances because I had no perspective, no judgment, and had a serious problem dealing with reality—as many people like me do." In fact, Elliott is now in favor of mandatory drug testing for performers.

His performance as a police chief on the trail of a missing woman in *Vanishing Act*, a 1986 made-for-television film, elicited the delicious observation from Tom Shales, the *Washington Post* critic, that "Gould proves again he is an ideal television actor. Cool and coiled and easy to take, he is also blessed with a face that is a carnival unto itself. Frame it in bunny-slipper earmuffs, and you have sure-fire stuff."

Sitting on a gray, upholstered chair in Room 718 at the Beverly Hilton—while members of the Saudi royal family were ensconced a few doors away, with a security guard sitting in the hallway—Elliott looks like the TV star he has become. He exudes charm and friendliness in his nondescript outfit of open white shirt, black pants, and brown, wing tip shoes.

He appeared as Dr. Howard Sheinfeld moonlighting in the emergency room of a Chicago hospital in the situation comedy *E/R*, in the 1985-86 CBS season. The following season he was back on the same network, in *Together We Stand*, a domestic comedy about a couple who adopt children.

What's his ambition at this time?

"I'm very ambitious. All the time it took me really to settle comfortably on myself, I've been able to define my ambition and my great life's desire in relation to everything that I've done, whatever will be done. I want to be a great-great-grandfather. And I would like for the children of the children's children to know me with my faculties and a conscious mind. Then I know that I will have achieved something. And to be able to pass time forward in relation to the truth."

Well, nobody accused Elliott of simplicity of thought. He is a thinker, he is introspective, and he is profound.

On his first trip to Israel, Elliott gained fresh insight into his Jewish soul. He went in 1984 to promote *Over the Brooklyn Bridge*, produced by Cannon Films, one of Hollywood's most powerful production companies, headed by Israeli movie moguls Menahem Golan and Yoram Globus.

The premiere was held at an air force base. The next night it was screened again in Tel Aviv. Elliott sat next to Prime Minister Shimon Peres and in front of Gen. Ariel Sharon. For lunch at the Knesset, he had gefilte fish, but found the horse radish too mild.

He spent a day at Kfar Chabad, the home of Lubavitch Hasidim in the Holy Land. He went to shul and wrapped *tefilin* around his arm and head for *shaharit*, the morning prayers. He went to Jerusalem, where he donned a *talit* and prayed at the Western Wall.

An avid sports fan, he was scheduled to kick out the first ball in a soccer match in Jerusalem. But he rejected the invitation because it was Shabbat. Elliott, whose faith in his Jewishness was immeasurably strengthened by his five-day sojourn in Israel, felt he could not violate the sanctity of the Sabbath.

As he was leaving my hotel room, Elliott showed me his black leather diary and appointment book. The inscription read:

> *To Ell*
> *May you fill these pages with days of happiness.*
> *Barbra*

Profile
Elliott Gould

Given Name: Elliott Goldstein.
Birthday: August 29, 1938.
Birthplace: Far Rockaway, Queens, N.Y.
Parents: Divorced; Bernard Goldstein lives in Tamarac, Florida; Lucille Goldstein in Los Angeles.
Siblings: None.
Height: 6' 3".
Weight: 214 lbs.
Eyes: Brown.
Hair: Brown.
Zodiac: Virgo.
Education: Seth Low Junior High School, Brooklyn; Professional Children's School, Manhattan.
Marriages: Barbra Streisand (mar. 1963, sep. 1969, div. 1971); Jennifer Bogart (1971-75, 1978-).
Children: Jason (b. 1967) by Barbra Streisand; Molly Safire (b. 1972) and Sam Bazooka (b. 1973) by Jennifer Bogart.
Personal Habits: Every now and then smoke.
Clubs: Friars.
Politics: Democrat.
Favorite Books: *Swiss Family Robinson*, *Charlotte's Webb*.
Favorite Movie: *Lies My Father Told Me*, especially where

Whoopi Goldberg is "not amused" by Elliott's clowning during filming of segment of CHABAD telethon in Los Angeles.

the little boy asks his *zaydeh* about the book, and he says he reads only one book, the Bible.

Favorite TV Shows: *I Love Lucy, The Goldbergs.*

Car: American Motors Eagle station wagon.

Pets: Two dogs, five cats.

Exercise: Tennis; jog in Will Rogers Park.

Charities: Israel Bonds, Chabad House.

Biggest Mistake: I don't think that way. I'm not a judge. I wouldn't change anything.

Biggest Irritant: My own blindness and persistence.

Hero: Different parts of different people. I look to purity, integrity, fidelity, bravery. But for me there is nobody.

Bad Habits: Talking too much.

Greatest Achievement: Having stuck with it and not having settled for anything less than everything in relationship to my beliefs.

Vacation Spot: My parents used to take me to the Catskills, and I'm becoming closer to nature now.

Kosher: No.

Synagogue: Any one I want to go to, Chabad, Bay Cities, any place.

Home: Brentwood, California.

I grew up in Manhattan,
which is ninety-five percent Jewish.
The neighborhood was mostly
Jewish and the kids I went to
school with were mostly Jewish.
But I had no Jewish education.

KEITH GORDON

A member of the new generation of young Hollywood actors, Keith Gordon left the exclusive Dalton School in the middle of his junior year to pursue his budding acting career.

Brilliant, fresh-faced and exuding high-power energy, Keith was sitting in the garden of my bungalow at the Beverly Hills Hotel, sipping bottled water from the kitchen inside the luxurious cabin, recounting the "frightening" experience of dropping out of school in the eleventh grade.

Since he was well ahead in credits, maintained an A-minus average, and was working more or less steadily as an actor, he obtained permission to take a light course load and do some study by correspondence. But after a couple of months, the administration balked, and insisted he stay in school full time and relinquish his acting jobs.

"I was incensed," Keith fumed. "I felt it was so unfair. My career was going well enough that I didn't want to give up the opportunity of growing up in the business. I knew it would be too hard to pick up again.

"I asked a lot of my friends and several college admissions people, and they said, 'Look, Harvard, Yale, and all those places will be a lot more impressed that you left school with an A-minus average and did not finish, than if you went out and got an equivalency degree, which looks like you kind of needed something to show that you finished high school.' So I just left."

With hindsight, Keith is not all that certain he would make the same choice. Having been out in the real world, he is well aware of how "dangerous and scary" it is, and how things can turn around.

"I don't know if I would be quite as brave. But with the bravado of a sixteen-year-old, it was pretty easy to do."

His father, Mark Gordon, a well-known drama teacher, actor and director, imparted lots of knowledge, but offered little encouragement at first. He knew the hardships and frustrations of the business and hoped his son would decide on some other line of work. Once he saw how well his son was doing and that he was able to make a living, he was proud.

"My parents are pleased and thrilled," Keith affirms. "But they're still worried about me. In the great Jewish tradition, they always want me to be even more successful."

His mother, Barbara Glenn of Queens, gave up acting to raise a family, and is now coming back as a producer. His father, also born in the Bronx, arrested Woody Allen in *Take the Money and Run,* and starred in the Broadway revival, *Of Mice and Men,* with James Earl Jones and Kevin Conway. He was in the original Compass Theater Company with Elaine May, Mike Nichols and Shelley Berman, which evolved into Second City.

The only time Keith worked with his father was when Dad directed him in *A Traveling Companion,* at Off-Broadway's Ensemble Studio Theater.

He received no formal training from his father, the drama teacher. But they would always sit around and talk. There were discussions on acting theory. They would act out little scenes in the apartment.

"It's like your father's a rabbi," Keith says. "If your father's a teacher, you're going to end up learning from him whether you want to or not. You either end up running away from the business, not wanting to do it, or absorbing a lot from him. It was the big subject of discussion in the house."

Pop even did some voice overs in *Static*, a movie which Keith helped write and produce, and starred in. It played at the Film Forum in New York in 1986.

Keith had always wanted to be a director, even before he set his sights on acting. He worked for free as an intern in the film department at the Museum of Modern Art after school. He eagerly learned about the film business while acting in several motion pictures. He played the pivotal role of Arnie Cunningham in John Carpenter's *Christine*, the computer whiz in Brian DePalma's *Dressed to Kill*, and Bob Fosse's young tap-dancing alter ego in *All That Jazz*. He spent forty weeks doing a small role in *Jaws 2* which turned out to be an education in filmmaking.

As for a Jewish education, it was nil. No synagogue attendance. Not even a bar mitzvah.

"On my father's side, there was deliberate choice about it," Keith explains. "His father, who came from Russia, wasn't at all a religious man, but very Jewish in terms of heritage and identity. He was part of that socialist movement that felt religion was the opiate of the people. Consequently, my father was brought up with an anti-religious bias.

"So I was not brought up religious at all. I was sort of aware of tradition, but it was never part of life.

"In a way, I am regretful of that. Although I'm not religious myself, I wish I knew more about the tradition. I have the feeling that at some point in my life I'm going to go back and make a real effort to know more of it."

Keith Gordon (**right**) *with Wally Ward and Dana Hill in* Com-
bat, *a 1986 NBC movie.*

Keith has been going with a non-Jewish screenwriter, Gloria Norris, for seven years. They are not in a hurry to get married. "We've both seen people we know have wonderful relationships, get married, and suddenly have the pressure of that change them," he says. "Both of us have fears of getting married. I assume we will, sooner or later."

They met under romantically contrived circumstances. She was a screenwriter of *Home Movies,* a student film at Sarah Lawrence College. Brian DePalma was the director of the project. Keith, who had left school at this point, went to audition for a role. He read a scene with Gloria. It was a love scene, about a guy asking an older girl out. It was appropriate, as Gloria is six years older than Keith.

"Sparks struck," he says. "Although it didn't actually develop into anything until several months later, nonetheless it was a romantic beginning for me."

Like many of the new crop of young Jewish screen stars, the only anti-Semitic confrontations Keith has experienced seem to be verbal.

When he worked on location in the South, young people would circle him and wonder: "You're really Jewish? What are you like? What do you people do? What kind of things do you eat? Do you believe in God, you people?"

"It's more confusion than active anti-Semitism," Keith observes.

Often he would get after-the-fact anti-Semitism. A person would utter a racial slur and then find out Keith is Jewish. The person would blurt out, "So you're Jewish? You know, I never expected one of you people to be nice."

Profile
Keith Gordon

Given Name: Keith Jonathan Gordon.
Birthday: February 3, 1961.
Birthplace: Bronx, N.Y.
Parents: Mark Gordon and Barbara Glenn.
Siblings: None.
Height: 5′9″.
Weight: 135 lbs.
Eyes: Brown.
Hair: Black.
Zodiac: Aquarius.
Education: Dalton School, Manhattan.
Marriages: None.
Children: None.
Interests: Movies, museums, theater, music, books.
Lifestyle: We go out a lot because neither Gloria nor I cook.
Habits: Don't smoke, don't drink, don't do drugs particularly.
Clubs: None.
Politics: You can't grow up Jewish in New York and not be Democrat. It's a tradition in our family.
First Job: At 13, I played a boy dying of kidney disease in an episode of *Medical Center.* They saved me.
Favorite Movie: *2001.* That was the film that got me thinking about making movies as a career.
Favorite TV Show: *Nightline, 60 Minutes.*

Jane Hoffman comforts an uncomfortable Keith Gordon on the bus to Albuquerque in STATIC.

Snack: Chocolate chip cookies.

Car: Toyota.

Pets: You're asking a New York Jewish boy if he has pets? We're all allergic to everything! But I did have lizards and frogs when I was growing up.

Exercise: Work out with a trainer on Nautilus machine.

Biggest Mistake: Turning down an offer to act in an independent underground film, *Dear Mr. Wonderful,* which was a nice movie.

Biggest Irritant: Lack of people wanting to make films, like *2001,* which are challenging and thought-provoking.

Heroes: Ghandi, Stanley Kubrick, Peter Sellers, Dustin Hoffman.

Bad Habits: Chronic insomnia, sugar food, lack of discipline.

Greatest Achievement: Getting *Static* made.

Vacation Spot: New places.

Kosher: No.

Synagogue: None.

Biggest Regret: Not knowing more about Jewish tradition. Also not having taken the time to grow up in certain ways. I feel sorry for the things I missed—not having much of a childhood or adolescence. I went from being 16 to being a grownup.

Home: Los Angeles.

My kids are now so assimilated
that they don't have what I had.
I feel bad about that.
I think that's a shame.

JOEL GREY

It is ironic. Joel, who was immersed in Jewish culture simply by being the son of Mickey Katz, the great dialect comedian and *Borscht Capades* star, was unable to pass on the tradition to his own son and daughter.

For if an ambitious greenhorn or Lower East Side pauper sought an easy way to assimilate into the American dream, he entered the world of show business. There he was given a new name, makeup for a new face, and new roles to act out. Those who opted to keep their foreign-sounding names and religious traditions played mainly to ethnic audiences. However, those who wanted to break out and appeal to a wider audience had to cast off their Eastern European baggage, the better to blend in with the all-American Anglo-Saxon community.

Mickey Katz's parents came from Russia. His father settled in Cleveland, Ohio, where he worked as a tailor, and was a devout Jew. During the Depression, Mickey was the only one in the family who was working. He put his brother through pharmaceutical school and payed for food for his mother and two sisters.

Mickey started out with the clarinet, playing in a performance of *Rhapsody in Blue* with the Cleveland Orchestra when he was sixteen. Later, he teamed up with Spike Jones. Then he started recording Yiddish versions of popular songs, such as *Haim on the Range, The Yiddish Mule Train* and *Duvit Crockett.* He made about seventy-five records for a limited market.

"He was a very timid performer," says Joel about his father, who died at seventy-five in 1985. "He was a performer in spite of himself. People loved him as a performer, but he really liked to be more in the background. He was not ever thrilled with having to get up and perform. It was thrust upon him. He made a record, it was a success, and there he was, with success thrust upon him. But he really had a great life."

Joel started out as Pud in a Cleveland Playhouse production of *On Borrowed Time* at age nine. Mickey had a vaudeville troupe which included his wife Grace and little Joel. His parents encouraged their son in show business. "Nothing could have made them happier," Joel says. "It was their dream that I become an actor."

While Joel attended Hebrew school in the evenings, his mind was on acting. He remembers coming back from Hebrew classes and stopping by at his grandfather's tailor shop. The windows were always steamed up because of the steam from the presses. Menachem Mendel the tailor would go over the Hebrew lessons and drill him.

Shortly after his bar mitzvah at Chebad Yerushalayim Synagogue, Joel and his family moved to California. There he went to Alexander Hamilton High School in Los Angeles. He was expelled for directing *Lady of Larkspur Lotion*, a Tennessee Williams play that proved too controversial at the time. Lady Larkspur was a drugstore remedy for crabs.

He took a job as a parking-lot attendant at the May Company. Joel was short, and the only uniform they had to give him came down to the floor. He looked like a kid in the Fiske Tire advertisement. The kid looked cute, but poor Joel looked ridiculous; the cars kept crashing into each other as the drivers went berserk with laughter. Joel was fired, but he did learn a bit about comedy.

Under the sunny skies of Southern California, this show business family became further assimilated. "My mother was never involved with Yiddishkeit," Joel says. "My father was more involved, though. But it got dissipated as we got older."

He did go to High Holiday services with his father. The elder Katz preferred the more modest surroundings of a small shul to the pompous cathedral-like structure of the modern temples.

"My father didn't like the baloney of the big stentorian rabbis who stand up there and pontificate about life. They were more English than the English people. He preferred to go to the more humble shul where men really come with their *talis*, a storefront on Beverly Boulevard where, when they blew the *shofar*, it went right through you. They really *davened*. He felt much more connected to that, and so did I."

When Joel was fifteen and a star in his father's *Borscht Capades* revue, he changed his name. Or rather, it was changed for him. Katz did not want audiences to think Joel got the job in the show because he was the boss's son. So he introduced the boy as Joel Kaye, as in Danny Kaye, whom he admired enormously. Katz's sister called herself Jeanne Kaye.

After the finale, Katz would conclude with these remarks aimed at the audience: "Joel thanks you, his mother thanks you, his grandmother thanks you; and I am his father." The listeners always were surprised.

"It's odd," Joel reflects. "He was using George M. Cohan's curtain speech to introduce me long before I ever knew I would play George M. Cohan in *George M!* on Broadway in 1968."

He also worked on stage, screen, television and night-clubs from Las Vegas to Atlantic City and in between. He was a teenage protege of Eddie Cantor, and appeared on his *Colgate Comedy Hour* in 1950. But, oh, how he hates those nightclub gigs. That is not what he was cut out to do, even though he does the best song-and-dance act in show business. He brought President Reagan and Nancy Reagan to their feet with an electrifying performance in a variety show at the Ford's Theater in Washington that was shown on CBS.

"I never wanted to work in nightclubs," he declares. "I never expected to do it. I had no preparation for it. The thing I expected to do, for which I trained, emotionally and technically, was to act. I was an actor when I was nine. That was always what I had in mind to do. That was the thing I was most comfortable doing. It was quite an irony that I was branded as a song-and-dance nightclub performer."

It was more of an irony that his breakthrough came when this crackerjack performer portrayed a song-and-dance master of ceremonies of the Kit Kat Klub in *Cabaret*, set in a decadent Berlin that ushered in the Nazi era. He was awarded a Tony for this Broadway hit in 1967 and an Oscar for his film version in 1972. "But this was from the perspective of acting," he maintains.

He was nominated for another Tony Award, for his portrayal of Jacobowsky in *The Grand Tour*, in 1979. After years of playing Irish, French, WASPs and Nazis, he finally got to do a Jewish character. He is proud of that role.

Even though he belongs to that vast group of Hollywood and Broadway folk who have strayed far from their Jewish roots while vying for success in the entertainment business, Joel still believes in the heritage of his father. No matter how much he has assimilated, he still feels connected.

He regrets that he could not pass on to his children the traditions of his grandfather, Menachem Mendel the tailor.

"I can't tell you why," he says. "It's being on the road, the lifestyle of trying to make it in this business, the traveling. There was a whole group of people that walked away."

He finds it hard to observe the holidays without family. One of the best things about Jewish holidays is that they preserve the family unit. But with a divorce (after twenty-five years of marriage to former actress Jo Wilder), the children grown up and in their own worlds, his mother and brother in Los Angeles, Joel finds it difficult to celebrate the Jewish holidays with the proper spirit.

It was no problem to observe the High Holidays when he was in *The Normal Heart* at the Public Theater in Greenwich Village, in 1985. He played the lead role in a play about the social and political impact of AIDS in New York during the early eighties.

The play's producer, the famed Joe Papp, invited Joel to join him for services on Rosh Hashanah and Yom Kippur at the Park East Synagogue on the Upper East Side. Joel rode from his home on the West Side. Papp, as is customary with Orthodox Jews who refrain from business and riding on religious holidays, walked the seventy-five blocks from his home in the Village to the synagogue on East Sixty-Seventh Street.

Producer James Nederlander, Carol Channing and Henry Fonda congratulate Joel Grey after his Broadway opening in THE GRAND TOUR.

PHOTO: TIM BOXER

Profile
Joel Grey

Given Name: Joel David Katz.
Birthday: April 11, 1932.
Birthplace: Cleveland, Ohio.
Parents: Meyer Myron "Mickey" Katz and Goldie "Grace" Epstein.
Siblings: Brother, Ron Katz, businessman in Los Angeles.
Height: 5′5″.
Weight: 125 lbs.
Eyes: Brown.
Hair: Brown.
Zodiac: Aries.
Education: Alexander Hamilton High School, Los Angeles.
Marriage: Jo Wilder (1958-83).
Children: Daughter, Jennifer (b. 1960), actress; and son, James Rico (b. 1964), chef.
Interests: Chamber music, ballet, tennis, art, cooking.
Personal Habits: Wine, non-smoker. I take care of myself.
Clubs: I'm not a joiner.
Politics: Democrat.
Favorite Book: Works by John Cheever.

Joel Grey and Mickey Katz delight the television audience with a father-son duet on Mike Douglas Show.

Favorite Movie: *How Green Was My Valley.*

Snack: Popcorn.

Car: None.

Pets: Two cats.

Hero: Jimmy Cagney and my father.

Favorite TV Show: The news.

Ambition: I need to play a character closer to who I am, a contemporary character, rather than a character role like the 75-year-old Korean martial arts expert in the film *Remo Williams: The Adventure Begins.*

Exercise: Gym.

Biggest Mistake: Selling a drawing I bought for $750 back to the dealer for twice the price, when I should have kept it because it is now worth $75,000.

Biggest Irritant: Excessive noise, especially from ghetto blasters in the park. Lack of consideration.

Bad Habits: Impatience.

Greatest Achievement: My children's sweetness.

Vacation Spot: Hawaii, France, Greece.

Home: Manhattan.

The Jews look after everybody.
The Jews are very big givers to the
Red Cross and the other charities.
Thank God for them,
because they have the same
tradition, that wonderful Jewish
tradition of tzedakah.

Monty Hall

There is no word for charity in Hebrew. Charity is looked upon as a duty; therefore, it is referred to as *tzedakah*, (righteousness). It is a moral and religious obligation of every Jew.

When I was growing up in Winnipeg, we kept several charity boxes in the kitchen, into which my mother would drop a few coins before pronouncing the Shabbat blessings over the candles on Friday evenings. Once a month I would trudge along several blocks, from one Jewish house to the next, collecting from those *pushkes* (charity boxes) for the Jewish National Fund.

Monty Hall does the same thing. He collects for charity on a much broader scope, flying from city to city, as America's premier master of ceremonies on the banquet circuit. He serves as *raconteur* at fund raisers for Variety Clubs, Israel Bonds, United Jewish Appeal, and hospitals all over the United States and Canada, and organizations fighting every disease imaginable. He has done so many benefits in Los Angeles alone, appearing in all the major hotels, that waiters think he is the maitre d'.

Since his wild game show, *Let's Make A Deal*, went off the air in 1977 after thirteen years, his main preoccupation has been charity. It did not start with the demise of his television program, however. He has been a dedicated fund raiser and devoted humanitarian right from the beginning of his career, when he first left Winnipeg after college to seek his fortune in Toronto. He immediately got involved with United Jewish Appeal, becoming president of the young men's division. He became active in Jewish and non-Jewish causes, including the Community Chest and Variety Clubs International. He got to California, at age 38, and joined the executive board of Variety. As he flourished and his fame grew, he would get ten calls a day to do charity events.

Many are called, but few respond. Monty responds. It has become his way of life. Everybody knows his reputation.

Fred MacMurray calls. He is being honored by the University of Southern California Film School. He says his night will be complete only if Monty would emcee. Monty opens his book and cheerfully exclaims, "Hey, I'm free that night. I'm going to do it for you, Fred."

Monty explains his philosophy: "I say yes first. Everybody else I know says no first. Then you have to grab him and twist his arm. I find it a lot easier that if you are free, do it. DO IT! Be a *mensch*, do it, help somebody."

A woman calls frantically from Albuquerque: "Israel Bonds is dying here. We can't get anybody. I need a star, I need a celebrity, I need you. Everybody I talked to says call Monty Hall. He's the one Jew who responds. He's the one who will come."

He comes to the aid of such Israeli hospitals as Hadassah and Tel Hashomer, as well as Tel Aviv University and the Israel Tennis Center. In the United States, three hospitals carry his name on a wing: Monty Hall Variety Children's Pavilion at Hahnemann Hospital in Philadelphia, Monty Hall Variety Center for Children at UCLA Medical Center in Los Angeles, Monty Hall Room for Pediatric Oncology Therapy at Johns Hopkins Medical Center in Baltimore.

"Every year I go out and raise fifteen to twenty million bucks. It's for cancer over here, leukemia over here, heart over here, multiple sclerosis over here. I call cards, I do an auction, I host a tennis tournament. For thirteen years, I've been doing a tennis tournament for the diabetes center at Cedars-Sinai Medical Center.

"These things take an awful lot out of you. You're either a comedian, a speechmaker or an auctioneer. I play all parts and write my own material. So it is very demanding. But if I am available I do it, that is my life."

You would think that the professionals who organize these events would know how to take care of their guest speaker. Nine times out of ten they are woefully ignorant. Their negligence and cavalier treatment angers Monty, who always comes well-prepared with a monologue and special stories about some of the guests.

"They don't have the time for the guest speaker. So they send one of the lay people to meet you at the airport. This person comes late. There is no limousine, the person is still car pooling, so you're in there with the kids. They dump you off in front of the hotel, with your bags on the street. You go up and it's not a suite, it's a room. It's a room so small you can hardly move in it. There's no fruit, there are no flowers, nothing. You come to the event. The dance floor is in front of the speaker. Guest speakers hate speaking to a dance floor. You put people in front and the dance floor in the back. They have candles six feet high on the tables so you're speaking through a picket fence. And they have five speakers precede you.

The sad part is that people take him for granted. They don't realize how much he prepares. He writes his own material, gathers stories about people in the audience, gets his tuxedo cleaned, puts gas in the car, pays the parking attendant. The kicker is he suffers indignities and charges nothing for his performance.

"I don't charge $20,000 like Henry Kissinger, because I am Monty Hall and Monty Hall charges nothing. He wants the money to stay with the charity.

"My public relations guy says, 'You are a fool. Charge these people $10,000. They'll love you. They'll appreciate you. They'll be scared to death.' But I can't do that because that's my life. Television and motion pictures come second. Above all, the family, of course. That's me and everybody in this town knows that's me."

Why this obsession with doing good deeds? What drives him beyond the limits of most other people in Hollywood? Why does he involve himself with so many charities when his celebrity colleagues take on just one favorite disease, if any?

"It starts in Winnipeg, where I was born. It starts with my maternal grandfather, coming from Pavoloch in the Ukraine, coming to Winnipeg and running a little fruit stand, becoming successful and sending for his family, and bringing over other people from Pavoloch. They formed the first shul, they built the Beth Jacob Synagogue, they started the Talmud Torah. My grandfather was one of the first presidents. They showed what Jews were all about. They organized the Hebrew Free Loan Society, Hebrew Sick Benefit Society, Immigrant Aid Society. Jews helped each other.

"That happened not only in Winnipeg but in every city where Jews settled. I speak for Jewish causes all over the United States and Canada and there are similar aid societies in every city I go to. Except Winnipeg is the one everybody talks about. They were the strongest and the best.

"There is probably a reason for that. Winnipeg was so isolated in the middle of the continent, we were a small minority and we had to protect ourselves from within. We did create these tremendous institutions and my grandfather, who came in 1901, was one of the original founders.

"Now you have that as your background, and then you have your mother. My mother was president of Young Judea, president of a Hadassah chapter in her early twenties and president of all the chapters in her late twenties, then vice president of the Western Canada region, then national chairman of Youth Aliyah in Canada.

"We were so poor we didn't have what to eat in the house. But my mother was still working for others, and she was helping the remnants of Jewry come to Palestine and have a place to live in those days. You learn by her example. Watching my mother in action, and my grandfather in his house where we lived half the time, these were the examples by which one lives and sets one's standards."

It is tradition, as Tevye says in *Fiddler on the Roof.*

"The Jews all have the same tradition of *tzedakah.* It's been with us for generations and generations and generations. I'm sure I've instilled that in my kids, because my son in San Francisco is already on the council of the Jewish Federation. He's working very hard on community relations. He has the same ethic, the same thing that was instilled in me. My daughters, I know, feel the same way."

Monty's paternal grandfather came from Brobruisk, Mogilev Province, Russia, and settled in Winnipeg in 1906. Monty's father Maurice Halparin owned a kosher butcher shop on Main Street in the North End, the Jewish part of town. Monty and his brother Robert would deliver meat to the customers.

Monty went to St. John's High School, as did most of the Jewish kids, including myself. He recently returned for a reunion with five thousand former St. John's students.

Naturally he was the master of ceremonies. He introduced himself to Senator S. I. Hayakawa of California.

"Senator, you are probably the most famous graduate of this high school."

"No," said Hayakawa. "You are the most famous graduate."

"Ah, but you became a United States Senator."

"But you," Hayakawa replied, "became a senator to the whole world."

Ironically, Monty, who grew up to become one of the most celebrated benefactors of the Hollywood community, was himself the recipient of charity when he was just out of high school.

His family was poor. His father could not afford to send him to college. He had three options:

1. Go into the Army.
2. Go into his father's butcher business.
3. Go into the wholesale clothing trade.

Monty got a job at a clothing wholesaler. One day a dapper gentleman named Max Freed told Mr. Halparin, "Did I see your son delivering a parcel? Why isn't he in college? Tell him to come and see me."

He asked Monty why he wasn't in college. Monty said he had to drop out after the first semester because he ran out of money.

Mr. Freed said, "If you want to go back, I'll give you the money providing you can live up to certain standards I'll set for you: Number One, I want you to keep an A average. Number Two, I want you to pay back every penny. Number Three, I want you to report to me every month. Number Four, I want you to do this for somebody else some day. And never tell anyone where you got the dough."

His benefactor invested $990 for three years, which paid for tuition, books, haircuts, lunches. Monty paid for the next two years by working nights at radio station CKRC, singing, announcing and sportscasting. He was president of the student body at the University of Manitoba and was graduated in 1945 with a bachelor of science degree.

Mr. Freed was perceived to be a playboy, very stylish, and very wealthy, having inherited the family clothing manufacturing business. He was a most unlikely person to make such a magnanimous gesture, or even such a generous loan for those times.

"In fact," Monty muses, "he showed something that all the rich people in town had not shown. They all knew me, they all knew my father, they all knew my mother was the top woman in Hadassah. Yet nobody stepped forward to say 'Can we help send your son to school'—tuition was $150 a semester. But this bachelor, this man-about-town, so unlikely a person to become concerned with me—you'd think he has to be a selfish individual, with the big cars and the flashy girls—the most unlikely person turned out to be the best-hearted, and I wasn't even close to him.

"These things don't happen very often. When I was sixteen, I was president of AZA, the B'nai B'rith youth organization. I'd shown all kinds of qualities. As it turned out, I was the first Jew to become president of the University of Manitoba student body. I mean, I had all these leadership qualities but nobody came forth to say to my dad, 'For the sake of a few hundred dollars this boy could go to college.' But this man did. He invested in me, and since then I have sent countless people through college. With my charity work, I raised four hundred million dollars. It would never have been done without Mr. Freed."

After college, Monty continued working at the radio station. One day his boss pulled out a map of Toronto and gave it to Monty. He said, "That's where you're going. I don't want you staying in Winnipeg. I want you to go to the big time. Don't stay here and become comfortable because you will always have a job here. That shouldn't be the limit of your ambitions. Go now."

Monty was twenty-one. He went home and told his folks he was leaving for Toronto. They were poor, had struggled for many years, and had little to offer their son.

Monty had gone through college on his own. He was making his own future. His parents kissed him and wished him good luck.

Looking back at the Toronto and New York experience, which consumed fifteen years of his productive life, Monty believes that it was a mistake. Toronto was not that great an opportunity, he found. He should have come directly to Los Angeles. "If I came here in the early days," he reflects, "I might have had a different future. This was a place for the young creative people. It was right here."

Rerouting his life to Toronto may have been a mistake, but Monty certainly has no regrets about marrying the woman he found there. "I married the right girl. We've had a terrific life and a terrific family."

He married the former Marilyn Plottel, an actress on CBC, for many years the only ingenue on Canadian radio. In recent years Marilyn Hall was associate producer of the television movie *A Woman Called Golda*, starring Ingrid Bergman. She was co-executive producer of the acclaimed television drama about Alzheimer's Disease, *Do You Remember Love*, starring Joanne Woodward and Richard Kiley.

"Marilyn is really booming in the movie business," Monty says. "She has four projects in the works, one of which is a movie to be made in Israel. We're bringing her company and my company together under one roof."

They have three children. Their oldest daughter is Joanna Gleason, whose first husband was Paul Gleason of the Los Angeles Civic Light Opera. She is now married to Michael Bennahum, president of Kaufman Astoria Studios in Queens, New York. An actress, she appeared on Broadway in *Social Security* and *I Love My Wife*.

Their second child is Richard Hall, executive producer of the news on Channel Two in Berkeley, California. His wife Wendy is the anchorwoman on the competing Channel Five.

Third child is Sharon Hall, recent graduate of Tufts University in Boston, where she majored in international relations. She will most likely join daddy's vocation rather than Henry Kissinger's business.

They live on Arden Drive in Beverly Hills. On one side is one of the foremost Mormons in the country, Dean Olsen, a former mayor of Beverly Hills. On the other side is Oscar Katz of Winnipeg, now in real estate. A few doors away are producer George Schlatter of *Laugh-In* fame, Mitzi Gaynor, Joe Bologna and Renee Taylor.

"You don't get to know all your neighbors," Monty notes. "I've been here twenty-four years. We live private lives. The difference is, when I lived in an apartment building in Winnipeg, we knew every neighbor. Our doors were never locked, and we walked into each other's apartments. It was a really friendly community. Today you put three bolts on your door. That's the difference in a couple of generations."

Taking a good overview of his life, he concludes: "Hey, I've been very lucky. Everything's been very good. I have a terrific family, I'm proud of each one of the kids, and my wife. I've achieved and done for mankind and for my Jewish people and for the whole country. How can I have regrets?"

Profile

Monty Hall

Given Name: Monty Halparin.
Birthday: August 25, 1925.
Birthplace: Winnipeg, Manitoba.
Parents: Rose Roosen and Maurice Halparin.
Siblings: Brother, Robert Hall, attorney in Toronto.
Height: 5'11".
Weight: 168 lbs.
Eyes: Hazel.
Hair: Brown.
Education: St. John's High School, Winnipeg; University of Manitoba, B.S., 1945.
Marriage: Marilyn Plottel, m. September 28, 1947.
Children: Daughters, Joanna Gleason, Sharon Hall; son, Richard Hall.
Interests: Golf, tennis.
Personal Habits: Gave up smoking the first day I taped *Let's Make A Deal*, December 16, 1963.
Clubs: Variety Clubs International.
Politics: Still a Canadian citizen, so I stay out of politics.
Social Life: Home entertainment with friends.
Favorite Books: Works by Chaim Potok, Bernard Malamud, Saul Bellow, but not Philip Roth who makes a mockery of his Jewishness.
Favorite Movie: *How Green Was My Valley*, because of the family ties in it that I love and respect.
Favorite TV Shows: *Naked City*, *Defenders*, the Paddy Chayefsky era, *Cagney and Lacey*, *Cheers*.
Snack: Fruit, at home, because we don't have pastries,

Monty Hall has just offered a shaggy "deal" on The All New Let's Make A Deal *TV show.*

but outside I'm a junk food addict, especially hamburgers (though they don't make *kukleten* like we had in Winnipeg).

Car: Cadillac; wife drives a Chrysler station wagon.

Pet: Dog, mongrel named Pepe.

Ambition: Working on the next show now that I've given up *Let's Make A Deal.*

Exercise: Walk three miles every morning.

Biggest Mistake: Staying with *Let's Make A Deal* too long; not going straight to Hollywood when I left Winnipeg.

Biggest Irritant: People who refer to me merely as 'the emcee of that mindless game show where people make fools of themselves,' instead of being regarded as a performer, actor, master of ceremonies for Variety and other charities.

Heroes: Bob Hope, Jack Benny, Henry Fonda, Jimmy Stewart.

Bad Habits: Junk food; taking on too much work.

Vacation Spot: Palm Springs.

Kosher: No.

Jewish Holidays: Have a Seder on Passover, go to shul on the High Holidays, say *kaddish* for my parents.

Honors: 500 plaques and awards including citations from Los Angeles and other major cities in the United States and Canada, tribute recorded in *Congressional Record*, Israel Bonds King David Award, Variety Clubs International Humanitarian Award.

The answer to anti-Semitism is education. You have to forgive somebody his poor upbringing. You cannot hold it against him. You can, but at the same time you have to understand.

Michele Lee

You can see the golf course of the Los Angeles Country Club through the French doors at one end of her living room. The glass doors open to her private woods, topped by a lonely palm tree straight ahead, and the requisite Tinseltown swimming pool at the right, below a patio just perfect for nighttime entertaining.

Through the open doors a stray cat strides onto the white wall-to-wall carpeting. Actually, it is a familiar cat, belonging to a neighbor across the street.

There is an art case piano, seventy-five years old, with gold leaf decoration. The piano is computerized. That means a music coach can play a piece on the piano while a computer device records it. Later, Michele will rehearse the piece by having the piano play it back again and again, until she learns how to play it.

The glass-framed photographs on the piano show the star with President Ronald Reagan, Betty Ford, Frank Sinatra, and Lee Strasberg.

Just inside the front door are three paintings by Israeli artists. One depicts fish at the seashore, another shows four Old World musicians, and another portrays several Hasidic types singing and dancing. She obtained them in various places—one in Denmark, one in a local gallery, one at an auction at Temple Sinai.

Her full-time secretary told me to make myself comfortable. Michele should be home any minute from her doctor's appointment. Nothing serious. But when Michele comes in, looking as beautiful and radiant in person as she does portraying Karen Fairgate MacKenzie on the CBS primetime soap series *Knots Landing,* she cannot sit.

"My back goes out once a year," she reveals. "I have a bad disc, although we will not talk about it."

I sip orange juice; Michele devours a plate of sandwiches, which were ordered from the Santa Glen Deli. She pours herself a cup of coffee from the sterling silver service and places it on the glass-topped mahogany table in front of the white sofa. Nearby is an armoire with her prized collection of Steuben glass.

It is a neat, ten-room house, well decorated with fine antique furniture which she collects with a discerning eye. Michele bought the house with James Farentino eighteen years ago, and kept it after their divorce.

Michele was brought up in a Jewish home where they went to Temple Beth Am during the holidays. She was raised on David Avenue, in a predominantly Jewish community in the Robertson-Pico area of Los Angeles, and attended schools that were three-quarters Jewish, but she nevertheless married out of her faith.

Michele and James Farentino met in 1962 in New York, when he was still married to Elizabeth Ashley. After his divorce, they met again several years later, and married in 1966.

"Jim really had no formal religious feelings," Michele says. "He wasn't a churchgoing Catholic. He had been going to Passover Seders for so many years before we married, he was used to it."

So Jim had no objection when his wife wanted to raise their only child in the Jewish tradition.

"From the beginning," Michele says, "Jim and I had decided to raise David in Judaism. It wasn't anything that my parents said. My parents never said anything about it to me. I just felt uncomfortable doing it any other way."

Michele's father Jack Dusick was a well-known Hollywood makeup artist. He worked on *Dr. Kildare, The F.B.I.* and other television shows at MGM, the same studio where Michele now films *Knots Landing.* Jack was born in New York, as was his wife Sylvia. They both died of heart attacks. Their parents came from Russia. Jack's parents died when Michele was young, so she was not close to them. Her maternal grandfather Saul Silverstein is ninety-six years old and lives in a retirement home in West Los Angeles. Michele and her brother Kenneth Dusick take their grandfather out every Sunday morning to Cantor's Delicatessen on Fairfax Avenue.

"Saul is a real Zionist," Michele says. "He would live in Israel now if he could. That's all he talks about."

Michele reveals that there were other intermarriages in the family, "which were quite accepted by my grandfather, which was quite interesting. He's a rather liberal old cuss. Especially for that age. Since he was young he accepted all kinds of people, all faiths. He was not prejudiced.

"He loves Farentino to this day. Talks about him. He sees Jim once in a while at social things. He says to him, 'You'll always be like a son to me.'"

After fifteen years, Michele and Jim divorced. The two other intermarriages in Michele's family also ended in divorce.

"It's true, you understand it when you're older what your parents mean when they try to keep you within their own kind," Michele says, "and you should, if at all possible. Hopefully you will fall in love with someone who has the same background, whether it is an emotional background, religious background, monetary or anything else, it helps. There is a difference. The thing is, you fight every-thing your parents tell you when you are younger."

The circle comes back. Michele is now going with a Jewish man, Fred Rappoport, Vice President of Special Events at CBS. They have been seeing each other for five years, and living together for three.

I wonder if she will marry, and she replies, "I am not looking forward to living with someone for fifteen years. I do believe in marriage. I mean, why live with someone for fifteen years without being married? I do believe in marriage."

I play devil's advocate. I remind her that some people believe a marriage will only ruin a good relationship.

"I think that's bullshit. I will tell you what I firmly believe. There is a difference between living together and being married. I don't care if you've been living together ten years. There's a level of commitment that comes with marriage that does not happen when you're only living together. It's an emotional thing.

"People are afraid of taking a gamble with two lives together. Either they've been burned by divorce or they've seen divorce around them or their parents have divorced. So they're afraid. Then what happens is you're living together, and you're not really on a level of commitment that hopefully, hopefully, two people come to."

I venture one last time an opinion that people living together seem to have far fewer domestic confrontations than married folk.

"I think you've got it all wrong," she retorts. "I think two people refrain from fighting with each other not because they are two separate wonderful individuals, but they're always afraid of losing the other person. It's a false, fraudulent kind of living. It's wrong. You hold back, afraid you'll lose the other person. You feel it's their house, their apartment, I don't have the right so I'll shut up. You have a feeling of independence that is not conducive to healthy

PHOTO:TIM BOXER

Michele Lee cuddles James Farentino at a glitzy Gotham gala during their marital years.

oneness of a relationship. There's a healthiness in the oneness, in the togetherness of matrimony."

So there.

Michele sees only the good side of life. She has always been that way. Even when she first started out, right after high school. Her first stage appearance was in *Vintage 60*, in which she sang a big number that proved to be a showstopper for eight months. Producer David Merrick brought her and the show to Broadway, but it lasted a mere eight performances. Characteristically, Michele saw only the good. She had made it from Los Angeles to Broadway in one audition.

A year later she was back on Broadway opposite Metropolitan Opera star Cesare Siepe in a new musical, *Bravo Giovanni*, for three months. Then came the big one. She starred opposite Robert Morse in the hit show *How to Succeed in Business Without Really Trying*, which won a 1962 Tony Award as Best Musical. She stayed with it for the full two-year run, and made her screen debut in the 1967 film version. It was back to Broadway in another smash, *Seesaw*, for which she was nominated for a 1973 Tony as Best Actress in a Musical. It was produced by Larry Kasha and the late restaurateur Joe Kipness. Michele played Gittel Mosca, a Jewish girl from the Bronx in love with a WASP attorney from Omaha (Ken Howard). Now she is in her eighth year of *Knots Landing* on television. She loves it.

She has never experienced anti-Semitism in show business. As she points out, "I belong to a community of artists in this industry that accepts and embraces Jewish people. Some of the most successful people in our industry are Jewish. A lot of businesspeople are Jewish and certainly half of our comedians are Jewish.

"I'm not about to feel the same kind of anti-Semitism that I would if I were a secretary living in the Midwest. Also, my celebrity probably keeps me insulated a little bit because, somehow, when you are a celebrity they accept you no matter what you are. Somehow the Jews are not bothered and the blacks are not bothered—provided you are a star."

Michele concludes that anti-Semitism in the world has become worse than when she was a little girl.

"I hate to say this, but as I look around the world I am frightened. I am a Jewish person who has actually had fantasies of, gee, what happens if my plane is hijacked...and I'm Jewish...I thought of all those things. A lot of Jewish people have thought the same things. I thought of going abroad, going to Paris. Think of the anti-Semitism that has been shown around the world. It's frightening. I don't remember feeling this way when I was younger. It's just getting so strange around the world."

Michele bridles when an anti-Semitic remark is thrown her way. She resents any prejudicial remark against any people, for that matter.

"I'm not only concerned about anti-Semitism. Being in California, for some reason people like to make derogatory remarks about Mexicans. I really get infuriated. Everything goes cold in me when anyone says derogatory things about anybody.

"Unfortunately, you look at these people and you know you can say to them—I do sometimes—that you're uncomfortable with that kind of joke. But they don't get it. That's because their parents didn't allow them to understand life on any other terms. Hopefully what we all can do is instill in our children the right values, because that's where our future is.

"I can show David my way of life, as my parents did with me. I can teach him how harmful derogatory statements and feelings are about all people. Hopefully David will pass that on to his children. We can solve the problem that way. It really is education. You have to forgive somebody their poor upbringing. You can't hold it against him. But at the same time, you have to understand."

Given Name: Michele Lee Dusick.
Birthday: June 24, 1942.
Birthplace: Los Angeles.
Parents: Jack and Sylvia Dusick.
Sibling: Kenneth Dusick, attorney, L.A.
Height: 5′8″.
Weight: 128 lbs.
Eyes: Brown.
Hair: Dark brown.
Education: Louis Pasteur Junior High School; Hamilton High School.
Marriage: James Farentino (mar. 1966, div. 1984).
Children: David (b. 1969).
Interests: Organizing 40 personal photo albums.
Personal Habits: Nonsmoker.
Clubs: Entertainment Industries Council (board member of Hollywood anti-drug abuse organization).
Favorite Book: *The Prophet.*
Favorite Movie: *Gone With The Wind.*
Favorite TV Show: *All In The Family.*
Snack: Anything Italian.

Profile
Michele Lee

Car: Two Mercedes plus an American Jeep.

Pet: Dalmatian—until she died.

Exercise: Exercycle, swimming.

Biggest Mistake: Taking for granted the success I enjoyed when I was in *Seesaw* and not taking full advantage of the situation.

Biggest Irritant: Being enclosed in an elevator with someone who recognizes you, and stares at you without saying hello.

Bad Habits: Talking too much at the wrong time.

Vacation Spot: Palm Springs, California.

Greatest Achievement: Learning more about myself.

Synagogue: Temple Sinai.

Honors: Woman of Achievement Award from Anti-Defamation League of B'nai B'rith (1984), Award for Outstanding Contribution to the Arts from Anti-Defamation League (1986), Arts and Entertainment Award from California Women's Commission on Alcoholism (1985).

Home: West Los Angeles.

Hal Linden and Ossie Davis cavort in I'M NOT RAPPAPORT.

PHOTO:MARTHA SWOPE

My father was a printer,
but a lover of music. He never
intended for any of us to become a
professional musician, but he made
sure that everybody had lessons
—me and my brother,
and all my cousins.
He always found the money
somehow.

Star *August 20, 1985*

Hal Linden

   It is a wonder that Hal's show biz marriage stayed intact
for so long, especially since the family's coffers were
generally empty during the years when he had to scrounge
from job to job until he finally achieved notoriety and
financial solvency at forty. It happened when he won the
Tony for Best Actor in 1971, in *The Rothschilds*. Hollywood TV producer Danny Arnold, who created *That Girl*
and *Bewitched*, spotted Hal in a Broadway musical and
hired him four years later to star in the title role of a new
detective series, *Barney Miller*. The show became a huge
hit on ABC, running from 1975 to 1982. At last the Linden
family's balance sheet stabilized.
   Hal met his wife, Frances Martin, when he got his first
acting job in 1955 at Cape Cod Melody Top summer stock
theater. She was the fiery red-haired dancer in the chorus.
The only show they did together on Broadway was *Bells
Are Ringing*. That was the first of eighteen New York

shows Hal appeared in. He understudied Sydney Chaplin and took over when he got the flu. When the show went on the road, Hal played the male lead opposite Judy Holliday. He married Frances while they toured with the show in 1958. Frances was Catholic. They married in church and raised their four children as Unitarians.

"In two months, there were six marriages in that show," Hal says. "Jean Stapleton married Bill Putch, a producer. Only our two marriages are still together."

Hal's Jewish heart is still together. Irv Kupcinet, the eminent columnist of the *Chicago Sun-Times*, had been after him for years to make an appearance at an Israel Bonds dinner. He finally relented, even though he was quite busy.

"Joey Bishop was there," Hal says. "Joey's first partner in nightclubs was Jack Soo. They were both scrounging at that time.

Jack Soo, of course, played Det. Nick Yemana on *Barney Miller* for three years until he died of cancer in 1979.

"Jack was on *Family Feud*," Hal continued, "and the question was, 'At what age does a boy become a man?' Most said twenty-one. Jack said thirteen. And you thought he was Japanese?"

So preoccupied with television movies and series (*Blacke's Magic*), a musical for cable (*I Do, I Do*), and touring with his nightclub act, it is not surprising that Hal has little time to devote to personal appearances at charity events. He receives requests constantly. One letter aroused his curiosity. It was from B'nai Zion, asking him to help raise money to build a rehabilitation center for disabled war veterans in Jerusalem.

"I stopped in my tracks," he recalls. "My father Charles Lipshitz, who came from Keidan, Lithuania, was a founding member of B'nai Zion in New York. I remember as a kid, there were meetings at our house, or Dad wouldn't be home because he'd go to the fraternal organization."

Hal went to Israel and looked over the organization's Beit Halochem rehabilitation center in Tel Aviv.

"A large portion of the population is disabled from so many wars. You can imagine how vast the problem is. What I saw was more than just a rehabilitation center. Israel is a summer country. Everybody goes to the beach— except those without limbs. So they created their own beach and pool at the center. It's like a country club for the disabled."

At the new Beit Halochem in Haifa, there is a plaque dedicated to the memory of Hal's father. Naturally Hal decided to tread in his father's footsteps and become involved with the humanitarian deeds of B'nai Zion.

When he was growing up in the East Bronx, little Harold had no idea he would end up an actor. His parents wanted Hal and brother Bernard to have business careers. Both boys were given musical education. Hal studied the clarinet and saxophone.

A cousin from Cleveland named Nat Gordon got a scholarship to Juilliard in Manhattan. He stayed at the Lipshitz home in the Bronx. His music proved contagious for Hal and Bernard.

Nat went on to play with the NBC Symphony, and most recently with the Detroit Symphony Orchestra, and to conduct the Birmingham (Michigan) Symphony. Bernard became a professor of music at Bowling Green State University in Ohio, where he also teaches viola.

While attending the High School of Music and Art in Manhattan, Harold Lipshitz would work nights as a clarinet player. Driving home one day, he passed through the New Jersey town of Linden.

Overnight, he became Hal Linden

"I could have driven through Nutley, New Jersey," he laughs. "What then—Hal Nutley?"

What's in a name, indeed? Is it not the talent that counts? It is certainly Hal's innate ability that got him an Emmy for his *FYI* series on television and a Tony for *The Rothschilds* on Broadway.

"All I need now is an Oscar for films," he says.

Profile
Hal Linden

Given Name: Harold Lipshitz.
Birthday: March 20, 1931.
Birthplace: East Bronx, N.Y.
Parents: Charles and Frances Lipshitz.
Sibling: Brother, Dr. Bernard Linden, music professor, Bowling Green State University, Ohio.
Height: 6' 1".
Weight: 185 lbs.
Eyes: Brown.
Hair: Gray-black.
Zodiac: Pisces.
Education: P.S. 98; High School of Music and Art; Queens College, music major; City College of New York, B.A. in business.
Marriage: Frances Martin (1958).
Children: Amelia Christine (b. 1960), Jennifer Dru (b. 1963), Nora Kathryn (b. 1966), Ian Martin (b. 1967).
Interests: Bridge, skiing, golf, tennis.
Honors: Tony Award for *The Rothschilds*, 1971.
Home: Brentwood, California.

I am a Jew. I will always be a Jew.

MELISSA MANCHESTER

Because she loves pickles, Melissa Manchester named her music publishing company the Rumanian Pickleworks.

The singer-songwriter was born in Manhattan. Her parents came from the Bronx. Her mother's mother was a native of Rzhishchev, near Kiev. It was in that Ukrainian village that her unusual family name originated.

As she recounted for me, there were two brothers who became orphans at an early age. The constable of the village gave them new names. He called one Simon, and the other Manchester because the youngster wore a royal-blue velvet suit known as Manchester blue. He was Melissa's great-great-grandfather.

Her professional life began at fifteen when she wrote commercial jingles. She also got jobs singing in the background on commercials.

Upon graduation from the High School for the Performing Arts (the school that is glorified in the television series
Fame), Melissa took a songwriting course at New York
University where the instructor was Paul Simon. Bette
Midler and her accompanist, Barry Manilow, hired Melissa
as a back-up singer (Harlette) in 1971. That gig included an
appearance at Carnegie Hall. Six months later she got a
record contract and was on her way solo. Her debut album
in 1973 was *Home To Myself*, containing some songs co-
written with Carole Bayer Sager. She played Carnegie Hall
as a headliner, fulfilling a childhood dream.

She continued to enthrall listeners with a string of highly
personal albums, among them *Don't Cry Out Loud*, *Help
Is On The Way*, *Better Days And Happy Endings*, recon-
firming her standing as singer and songwriter. Her rock
rendition of *You Should Hear How She Talks About You*
won her a Grammy as Best Female Vocalist in 1982.

When Melissa tours, it becomes a family affair. Her
father, who played bassoon for twenty-nine years at the
Metropolitan Opera, accompanies her on the road. Her
mother Ruth helps design the costumes. Her sister Claudia
is one of the three back-up singers. Claudia's husband,
Steve Cagan, is the orchestra conductor.

At nineteen, Melissa married Larry Brezner in a Reform
wedding which she wrote. He served as her personal manager. Seven years later, divorce ended both relationships.

"You don't get over the trauma of a breakup for a long
time," she says. "Without love, all the hard work becomes
an exercise in futility."

She found love at last, again within her organization. In
1982 she married her tour director, Kevin de Remer.

Melissa has come a long way from the Bronx where she
grew up. She now lives in Beachwood Canyon in Los
Angeles, where the HOLLYWOOD sign stands. "My house is
under the D," she says.

She still remembers her roots back east. "There's a
memorial to my father's father in the Ocean Beach Synagogue on Fire Island."

Profile

Melissa Manchester

Given Name: Melissa Manchester.
Birthday: February 15, 1951.
Birthplace: New York City.
Parents: Ruth and David Manchester.
Height: 5'4".
Eyes: Brown.
Hair: Brown.
Marriages: Larry Brezner, 1970-77; Kevin de Remer, 1982.
Children: None.
Home: Los Angeles.

In New York,
they think I am a Hollywood star.
In Hollywood, they think I am this
underground New York actress.
Which more or less puts me in
Kansas City, where they say,
I wonder if she is Jewish.

Sylvia Miles

This is one actress who is highly conscious of the importance of being seen, not only at the agents' offices, but at the restaurants and Broadway openings where her peers are gathered. Since she appears as different characters in different films and plays, how will producers and directors know she is right for a future role if she doesn't keep her face in the public eye? Having seen her as a seventy-five-year-old woman in *Farewell My Lovely*, employers won't realize she was also a thirty-five-year-old in something else. It's when they see the ubiquitous Sylvia in person at openings and premieres that they realize she is a fine character actress who can take on diverse roles.

Because she is seen everywhere, the gossipists accuse her of being a party person, completely ignoring the fact that she is one of our better performers with an Academy Award nomination for *Midnight Cowboy*.

"They used to say, 'the omnipresent Sylvia Miles,'" she laments. "They'd say I'd go to the opening of an envelope. Now they say it about Andy Warhol. They used to say I ordered a cup of coffee at Joe Allen's. Now they say it about Bette Midler.

"These interviewers, they're on the job a year or two, and they've been told Sylvia Miles goes to a lot of parties, and suddenly they disassociate me from what I am and what I do and now I have become a party person. That's ridiculous."

Sylvia insists she does not go out unless there is a reason. If she goes to Ruth Warrick's birthday party, it is because Ruth is a friend with whom she worked on *All My Children*. "I socialized with her. Why shouldn't I go to her birthday party?"

For an entire year when Sylvia was working in England, friends would send her newspaper clippings about her alleged appearances at Studio 54 and being seen at other popular hangouts. While she was away in Israel for a month filming *Sleeping Beauty*, the press insisted she was participating in Hands Across America. She is incensed at the inaccuracies of the gossip columnists who perpetuate her as a party person.

Sylvia is fun to be with. She is a fun loving person. If she can further her career by going out to celebrity parties, well, why not? "I've tried to keep my eye on the stars," she says. "I've tried not to compromise myself. I've tried to make a buck at my art in a hard, tough world."

And if there are those who love to denigrate her talent and ambition, she will understand. Nonetheless, it aggravates her. Because there is no recourse, no redress, it really irritates her.

"But I don't have to get back at anybody. Time itself will do that. Time wounds all heels."

Sylvia is a devoted New Yorker. She was born here and named after Sylvia Sidney. Her father Reuben Lee was a furniture manufacturer at 178 Prince Street. She was two years old when her parents divorced. She was raised by her Jewish father and Catholic stepmother in Greenwich Village.

She was not raised in any religion but, living in an Italian section of the city, she was more aware of Catholic ritual than Jewish rites. She was always there for the festive San Gennaro street galas. Most people thought she was Italian.

Nevertheless she always accepted her Jewish heritage as a privilege. By choice she always felt Jewish, even though she never had a Jewish home when she was growing up.

"I did not take advantage of the fact that I was not brought up to be a Jew, to say, 'Oh I'm not a Jew,'" she says. "I felt very strongly that I was privileged to be a Jew because it was part of the hidden source of my desire to better myself and to aspire as an artist. I always felt fed by the fountain of my heritage."

It is remarkable that, although not raised particularly Jewish, Sylvia came to the realization of who she was completely on her own efforts. "I was an intellectual," she explains. "At a very young age I was aware of my heritage as an American, my heritage as a Jew, my heritage as a woman. I was a resolute native of New York. I was determined to be sustained in my own city by myself."

After she was graduated from Washington Irving High School, she went to Pratt Institute in Brooklyn to study stage design with Norman Bel Geddes, father of Barbara Bel Geddes, who is the matriarch Miss Ellie on *Dallas*.

At fifteen she got a summer job as a set designer at a theater on Long Island. They sent her out to get some props. She paid ninety dollars for them and presented the bill to the producer. He was shocked.

"You're not supposed to pay for props," he said. "You're supposed to rent or borrow and give them billing."

"But where's my ninety dollars?" the youngster demanded.

"Tell you what. I'm going to give you a part in the play and I'll give you ninety dollars and that's how you'll pay."

PHOTO:TIM BOXER

Sylvia Miles, surrounded by memorabilia of her theatrical career, relaxes in her posh condominium on Central Park South.

Sylvia abandoned her short-lived career as a stage designer and became an actress. She does not remember what play it was, but she was playing an old man of eighty. The other players waited a long time as she hobbled across the stage, very slowly, like an elderly man.

"It took so long to go across the stage it felt good," she says.

Having lived in the Big Apple all her life, Sylvia feels a proprietary relationship to her beloved city. It distresses her to see the eager, ambitious, aspiring troupers swooping into the city year after year and fighting to displace the people already working here.

"It has always been," she says, "that everybody who comes here, no matter who is in the forefront when they arrive—the person in the forefront could only have been famous two weeks—the immediate thing is to get that person out and they should take over. It's a constant competitive thing with all the people who come to New York. Which is really why the people who live here, who were born here and raised here, find it necessary to flee, because they don't have the benefit of their birthright.

"The benefit of your birthright is to be able to live where you were born, stay there and raise your family and be an accredited member of the community.

"We're not allowed to do that because of this being a piratical culture where people come in from the outside, the commuters, to make their living here, loot the city, and then take the train and go home somewhere else.

"What about me? I was born here. I've paid my taxes all my life. I've been a credit to my profession and to my city. I've been an interested and participating member of my community. I find it very disturbing that I am not given the due that I feel is mine.

"They would say I am not a member of the establishment. I am the original establishment—I was born here.

"I'm considered a maverick when actually I'm a conservative human being. I'm mistaken for being a bizarre, oddball downtowner. I was born downtown, but now I live on Central Park South."

Sylvia's one-bedroom apartment looks out on a grand panorama of Central Park. Every square inch of her walls is covered with mementoes of her various movies and plays from around the world. Posters, masks, costumes, framed invitations, autographed photos, art work, props and other artifacts of a life on stage and screen are festooned on the walls, over windows, on the tables and chairs, in the closet, on the closet doors inside and out, in the bathroom and on the floors, in trunks and suitcases and drawers. She ought to charge her visitors an entrance fee to marvel over the display of her personal museum.

There is even a collection of stuffed animals to remind one of her work. There's an iguana from *The Night of the Iguana*. There is a leather terrier from another play, and a cat from *The Owl and the Pussycat*. A trunk next to the door contains newspaper clippings about her and her many projects. She even has Michael Jackson's white glove to remind her of the party where they met.

"You can see my life right around here," she says. "Every piece here came from an experience theatrically, or in the course of my career. Tennessee Williams gave me those plaster masks made of his face. They look like him, so real."

Sylvia used to describe her apartment as a wardrobe trunk with a view. Now she calls it a drawer with a view. The apartment hasn't shrunk. Her incredible collecting has just escalated enormously. There is simply no space to entertain guests at tea. She is fortunate the Russian Tea Room is nearby.

Sylvia went to Israel for the first time in her life when Cannon Films offered her a role in *Sleeping Beauty*. Two Israeli film producers, Menahem Golan and his cousin Yoram Globus, have developed over a few short years into two of Hollywood's foremost movie moguls. They are currently filming a series of fairy tales at their studios in Israel. Amy Irving, the wife of Steven Spielberg, starred in the first one, *Rumpelstiltskin.* Her brother David Irving directed it. He also directed *Sleeping Beauty,* the second tale to be filmed. Sylvia plays the Evil Fairy of Red, Morgan Fairchild is the Queen, Shai K. Ophir is the Master Elf, and Tahnee Welch (Raquel Welch's daughter) is Sleeping Beauty.

"I had no idea Israel is so beautiful," Sylvia says. "It's like a garden spot. People told me Tel Aviv is a very busy city and I wouldn't like it, but I would love Jerusalem.

"Well, I found Jerusalem beautiful, but I found Tel Aviv very exciting because it has the beauty of a resort and the hubbub of a big city. People were very friendly. It was very cosmopolitan. In the afternoon people sat at the cafes. I loved how the old people were treated, with reverence. It was very safe there, and very positive.

"It is also very clean there. So many trees. All those trees that I heard about all those years that people donated to the Jewish National Fund. I was sorry I didn't have a specific tree that I could have gone to—this is my tree."

Luminaries Hedy Lamarr and Sylvia Miles at a New York party.

PHOTO:TIM BOXER

Profile
Sylvia Miles

Given Name: Sylvia Lee.
Birthday: September 9.
Birthplace: New York City.
Parents: Reuben Lee and Belle Fellman.
Siblings: Sister, Thelma.
Height: 5'5".
Weight: 130 lbs.
Eyes: Brown.
Hair: Blond.
Zodiac: Virgo.
Education: Washington Irving High School; Pratt Institute.
Marriages: First marriage at 16 to William Miles; second marriage at 18 to George Price, a documentary producer; third marriage at 25 to radio personality Ted Brown, 1963-68.
Children: None.
Interests: Theatrical and movie memorabilia.
Personal Habits: Smoke two or three cigarettes a day; don't drink unless it's someone's birthday.
Clubs: Manhattan Chess Club, Chess Federation of America, Writers and Artists for Peace in the Middle East.
Favorite Books: Works of Jane Austen, Henry James.
Favorite Movie: *Abbott and Costello Meet the Wolfman and Frankenstein.*

Snack: The bane of my existence, pizza.

Car: None.

Pets: None.

Ambition: Keep the wrinkles in your belly, always stay hungry, never get too satisfied, or it takes away the desire, the yearning and the dream of going ahead and achieving greater heights.

Exercise: Calisthenics.

Favorite TV Show: *Good Morning America* on ABC.

Charities: Actors Fund, Actors Studio, Cancer Care, Muscular Dystrophy, Central Park preservation.

Biggest Mistake: I didn't take a larger apartment before the rents changed.

Biggest Irritant: I'm considered a maverick when actually I am a conservative human being. I'm mistaken for being a bizarre, oddball downtowner. I was born downtown, but now I live on Central Park South.

Politics: I'm a rugged individual.

Hero: Lee Strasberg.

Vacation Spot: My next movie location.

Kosher: No.

Jewish Holidays: Seders with close friends.

Synagogue: None.

Home: New York City.

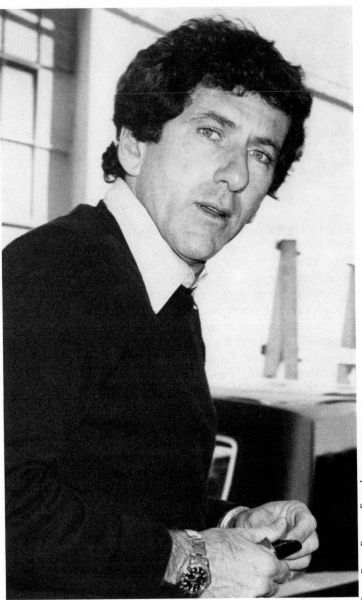

I have a real Jewish mother.
She sees me on television and,
instead of talking about my
performance, would say,
"I didn't like the way your hair
was cut."
She used to send me letters with
instructions
on how to open a jar of coffee.

BARRY NEWMAN

With such a Jewish mother, it is amazing Barry Newman has never been married. Every time he came close, he could never make the commitment. He remains the sole single guy among his close friends. He has even been in therapy, but the therapist told him, "Who says you have to be married?"

When I dropped in on him at his Beverly Hills home, he was feeling low. He had a terrible battle with his girlfriend. She found a letter from a female fan.

"It was one of those things," Barry says, "that if you did as a comedy sketch would have been hilarious."

It seems some ardent admirer sent him a strange letter pleading, "We should be together." Barry's girlfriend did not appreciate that famous personalities get all types of odd letters from the vast public. She stormed out of the house.

Barry was in no mood to fight. His right leg was in a cast. He had visited a buddy in Malibu. He climbed up a rock formation to get some sun. Then he jumped down and hit the cement walk, breaking his ankle.

The letter incident was not the first time Barry got into hot water with a lady. In 1979, *Cosmopolitan* interviewed six male sex symbols including Richard Burton, Jim Brown and Barry. Leave it to Barry to state, in jest, that a woman's place is in the home. The magazine labeled him a male chauvinist supreme.

"I got hate mail from women," he recalls in horror. "But I'm not like that at all. My personal manager was a woman, my publicist was a woman, two of my agents were women, and my mother's a woman.

"I am not a male chauvinist, not in any intellectual sense. But I am only in a sexual context. Women want their males to be dominant. You ask twenty-one out of twenty-four girls—and they would say yes."

Barry has been enamored of women since the days his father Carl operated the famed Latin Quarter in Boston. During the week he would be at the Boston Latin School, the oldest public school in the country. On Sundays he would be at his father's nightclub watching the chorus girls rehearse.

"I'd see all the sexy showgirls. I'd go back to school Monday and I didn't know what I was doing. It was wild. I'd be sitting there, looking out the window, thinking of a showgirl named Lillian Lawrence whom my saxophone teacher was dating. And the history teacher would say, 'Newman, wake up. We're talking about Mycenaean civilization.' It was all I could think about."

Barry played saxophone through high school and college. He would play at bar mitzvahs and weddings in bands booked by Gene Dennis of Brookline. A saxophone player himself, Dennis put musicians together for any affair and had twenty bands going every weekend.

When Barry got to Brandeis University, acting was furthest from his mind. He attributes that to his father's influence.

"My father was very down on performers. He was a Mike Todd kind of character. He said they never tip, they're lowlife, they never appreciate anything, they never picked up a tab in their life.

"There was a wonderful comic working at the club in the fifties named Joey Carter. He was a young comic, not from my dad's era, and was getting only seven hundred and fifty a week. My dad didn't like him at all, didn't laugh. Danny Thomas was getting seventy-five hundred a week. Boy, did my dad laugh!

"That taught me a lesson. The more you demand, the more money you get for your work, the more respect they have for you. If you get that much money, then you must be pretty good."

His biggest influence in college was an anthropology professor named Bernard Mishkin. "He was the world's foremost authority on the Plains Indians," Barry says. "He was a strange guy. He chewed coca leaves. He drove around in a Porsche and would run down to New York where he was dating a ballerina. This is a professor? Wow!"

Can a fellow make a living in anthropology? Barry hoped to work for a large corporation.

"For example, if you were Schlitz Beer, and you wanted to find out how best to sell your beer to a rural community in Maine, you would hire an anthropologist. The psychologist works with the sum total of the society. So there is a commercial aspect to it. Yet you still go into the various communities of the world to study them."

Barry wrote his thesis on a particular aspect of a minority group in the United States, the Italian Mafia.

At Brandeis, a noted director, Elliott Silverstein, was brought in from Yale to stage *Our Town*. He observed Barry putting on a comedy skit for the boys in the dormitory, a cancer benefit in memory of a fellow student. When the person assigned to play the stage manager in *Our Town* did not show up, Silverstein recruited Barry for the role.

With that auspicious beginning, his dramatic career took off. It was not without its highs and lows. For instance, in 1970 he was offered a role in the motion picture *M*A*S*H*.

It was being produced by Otto Preminger's brother Ingo. He was a literary agent and this was his first production. Barry turned it down. "I didn't realize it would turn out to be an improvisation, because of the director, Robert Altman," Barry says ruefully. It also turned out to be a smash hit, leading to the wildly popular television series.

You can be sure Barry did not reject Ingo Preminger's follow-up film. He willingly signed on for *The Salzburg Connection.* It quickly proved to be a disaster.

No matter. Barry appeared in other motion pictures and television movies. His biggest success was starring as the lawyer in the TV series *Petrocelli* from 1974-76. He created the role in a 1970 movie called *The Lawyer.*

At home Barry does not keep kosher. In fact, he has never eaten a meal in the house. "I don't cook," he says. "I eat every meal out. In the refrigerator I have cranberry juice and fruit. That's it. Even at my apartment in New York, when I have a guest over who wants a cup of coffee, I call the Carnegie Deli and say, send over some containers of coffee."

He did not have a kosher home growing up. However, his mother refused to keep ham or bacon in the house.

"My dad and I would have to go out and eat breakfast somewhere. Later in life she brought bacon and ham into the house."

Barry learned to appreciate his cultural heritage, though he did not have a religious upbringing. After his bar mitzvah, he attended temple for two or three Saturdays, and that was it for religion.

"My mother would light the Friday night candles. But as we got older, and the family became moderately successful and more affluent, she didn't do it as much."

Barry Newman and co-star Susan Howard of PETROCELLI.

Given Name: Barry Foster Newman. (Mother was in love with a Harvard football player, Barry Wood. Foster, I have no idea where it came from.)

Birthday: November 7, 1938.

Birthplace: Boston.

Parents: Sarah came from Russia at 10 months old; Carl came from Vienna at 6.

Sibling: Brother, Edmund Newman, doctor, of Scarsdale, N.Y.

Height: 6'.

Weight: 166 lbs.

Eyes: Green-blue.

Hair: Brown, turning gray.

Education: Boston Latin School; Brandeis University.

Marriage: None.

Children: None.

Clubs: None.

Politics: Independent.

Social Life: Date a lot. I'm not a swinger, don't go to discos, hate loud music. I go out for a good meal, theater, music, a quiet social evening.

Favorite Book: Lee Iacocca's autobiography.

Favorite Movies: *Sweet Smell of Success, Viva Zapata, On The Waterfront.*

Favorite TV Show: *Petrocelli.*

Snack: Fruit.

Profile

Barry Newman

Car: Classic 1957 Mercedes 190SL convertible and a little Honda.

Pets: None.

Ambition: I want to get back into the film business. I'm at the top of the television ladder, but at the bottom of the motion picture ladder.

Charities: Marion Frostig Center for mentally-handicapped children; Salvation Army.

Biggest Irritant: Women who interrupt a conversation and have to insert themselves into the conversation without adding anything to it. I've seen it in friends' wives; I hate that.

Hero: Albert Einstein.

Greatest Achievement: What I've enjoyed as an achievement is the fact that as an actor, it's amazing to me that we can leave something behind.

Bad Habits: Impatience and intolerance. I'm intolerant of stupidity.

Vacation Spot: Hawaii.

Kosher: No.

Synagogue: Synagogue for the Performing Arts, L.A.

Biggest Regret: I didn't spend enough time with my father when I could have. We were very close. I was busy with my career.

Home: Beverly Hills; New York City.

A "down on the Earth" Leonard Nimoy relaxes in N.Y.

I would never change my name
because I felt that I would like my
family to be a part of any success I
had. I do not want to disconnect
from my family.

LEONARD NIMOY

He put on those outlandish pointy ears and became a sensation with youthful sci-fi fans and a veritable sex object with the ladies. His Vulcan ears proved irresistible to the female viewers of NBC's *Star Trek*. Female visitors on the set of the U.S.S. Enterprise at Desilu Studios simply had to reach out and touch those sexy ears.

The years were 1966-69 when two Jewish actors, Leonard Nimoy and William Shatner, dominated the galaxy. When the show went into syndication, the two stars began to shine, and they reigned as cult heroes to a generation of Trekkies. That is no mean feat in view of the fact that science fiction had heretofore been spectacularly unsuccessful as a television format. It still is.

While Leonard and the producer decided that Dr. Spock should be greenish, with short hair in bangs and pointed ears, it was Leonard who reached back into Jewish tradition to create the unique Vulcan greeting. The Vulcan hand symbol is a direct steal of the priestly blessing in the Holy Temple of ancient Jerusalem, still employed by present-day *kohanim* in the synagogue on Jewish holidays. Today's *kohanim* bless the congregation by spreading their hands outward. The thumb is stretched wide, the index and middle fingers are held close together, away from the ring finger and little finger which are held close together. One interpretation of this hand symbol is that it forms the Hebrew letter *shin*, the first letter in the word *shalom* (peace). Thus postured, the *kohanim* utter the three-fold biblical blessing that concludes with, "The Lord turn His countenance toward you and grant you peace."

It took seventeen years of hard labor in the vineyards of Hollywood before Leonard achieved a measure of success on the small screen. He feels those lean years could have been avoided had he set his sights on Manhattan rather than Los Angeles when he bolted Boston College at eighteen. Going to L.A. after he left home was the biggest mistake he made at the beginning of his career.

I am sitting in his office on the Paramount lot hearing Leonard define his one mistake. He interrupts an extremely hectic day of post-production of the latest Trekkie epic, *Star Trek IV: The Voyage Home,* to welcome me. Besides continuing his character of Dr. Spock, he also is director of the film.

There is a large erector set on the table. "I liked to build things when I was a kid," he says. "I used to have an erector set. I mentioned that on a talk show and somebody sent me this set." The perks of the trade.

The coffee table holds several books, among them *Hannah Senesh: Her Life and Diary,* with introduction by Abba Eban. He says he was looking through books like this in preparing a speech he gave at a luncheon honoring Mel Mermelstein, hosted by Holocaust survivors at the Beverly Hilton. Mermelstein is the Holocaust survivor who won a court case against the Institute for Historical

Review, after they offered $50,000 to anyone who could prove that Jews were gassed at Auschwitz. Leonard met with Mermelstein several times and is developing a television movie based on his experiences.

Pacing the floor nervously—he has to get back to the editing room where he has been spending most of his days —Leonard recounts his decision to go west that he regrets to this day.

Born and bred in Boston, Leonard grew up in a kosher home. His parents Max and Dora came from Zaslav, a small Ukrainian town near the Polish border. They knew each other, but came to the United States separately in the mid-twenties. She came with her parents directly to Boston. Max arrived in New York first, where he lived for a short time with relatives, then moved to Boston where he was reacquainted with Dora. He was a barber.

Leonard and his brother Melvin went to Hebrew school every day after public school.

"My grandmother was the most religious in our family. We all lived together until we split up into two apartments in the same building. My grandmother baked *challah* every Friday which we had for the weekend, and lit the candles every Friday night. I went to services for a while on Saturday mornings. I wasn't really committed to a religious life. I was very much attached to the social and cultural aspects of Judaism, but not terribly attached to the religious aspects."

He was a member of the B'nai B'rith Youth Organization, AZA. The group presented him with its Sam Beber Award as Distinguished Alumnus in 1985. Now he belongs to the Benjamin Cardozo Chapter of B'nai B'rith, named for the Supreme Court Justice.

Acting became an early obsession when, at eight, he played Hansel in a Boston settlement house's Elizabeth Peabody Theater production of the musical *Hansel and Gretel.* For the next nine years he continued to act on stage and radio. At seventeen he performed in *Awake and Sing* at the Peabody, directed by Harvard law student Boris Sagal. This is the same Sagal who, after starting out as an actor in Yiddish theater, became an eminent film director whose television credits include *Masada*, *The Diary of Anne Frank* and *Rich Man, Poor Man.* His career ended tragically. He died on a movie set when he accidentally walked into the revved up blades of a helicopter.

Due to his latest performance at the Peabody, Leonard was given a two-month summer scholarship in drama at Boston College. He then applied and was accepted for admission to the Pasadena Playhouse. He was eighteen. Strangely enough, that turned out to be the biggest mistake of his career.

"It was not a good idea," he reveals. "I should have gone to New York. The Pasadena Playhouse was almost closing, on its last legs, when I got there. I didn't realize that until I arrived. I wasn't very happy with the place. I could have picked up and gone back to New York but I decided to stick it out. I liked the weather."

Leonard was sorry he was enticed by the tall palm trees swaying on the sunny boulevards. For what he really looked forward to was a richer theatrical grounding. He did not find that when he came to Los Angeles in 1949. Theater then was just at its bare beginnings.

"But it worked out fine," he reflects. A year after he arrived in Hollywood, he made his first television appearance in an NBC situation comedy, *The Pinky Lee Show* (real name: Pincus Leff). He played a gangster in a comedy sketch on this live TV show. The next year he made his movie debut in *Queen for a Day.* The year after that he got the title role in a motion picture, *Kid Monk Baroni*, playing an Italian boxer with a disfigured face.

After completing this little B movie, *Kid Monk Baroni*, on which he was getting introductory billing, Leonard was faced with the prospect of changing his name. The producer told him, "If you ever want to change your name, now would be the time to do it."

"I hardly gave it any thought," Leonard recalls. "I thought it was an interesting name, an unusual name. I also felt that I would like my family to be a part of any success that I had. I did not want to disconnect from my family."

Over the years he developed into a fine character actor, an excellent drama teacher and a great director.

On the screen, he starred in *The Balcony* (1963) and *Invasion of the Body Snatchers* (1978). On television, he portrayed the character Paris for two years on *Mission Impossible* on CBS, hosted *In Search Of* for ten years in syndication, and made numerous other appearances in series and TV movies. On Broadway, he starred in *Full Circle* (1973) and *Equus* (1977). As a young man, he appeared with the great Maurice Schwartz in the English language adaptation of Sholom Aleichem's *Hard to Be a Jew* (1953) at the long-defunct Hollywood Civic Playhouse.

That is how Leonard met his wife. A replacement was needed for the ingenue in *Hard to Be a Jew*. Among the actresses who auditioned was a beautiful, intelligent woman named Sandi Zober. She came from Cordova, Alaska, the only Jewish family there. She failed to win the role, but gained a better prize—Leonard Nimoy for a husband. They have two children. Their daughter Julie is a housewife and mother living in Los Angeles. Their son Adam is an attorney and counts his father as one of his prime clients.

Behind that craggy face is the mind of a poet. Leonard has published a number of books of poetry, three of which include his own photographs. He is an accomplished photographer, specializing in black-and-white still lifes, landscapes and nature, but not portraiture. He published his first poetry book in 1973, and for a while he did one a year. Recently he has become too busy, but the interest is still there.

Another hobby was flying. He owned a single engine, four-seater for ten years, but not anymore—again, too busy.

In 1971, when he appeared in a Cape Cod production of *Fiddler on the Roof* in Hyannis, a Boston friend flew down to pick Leonard up for a ride. He got Leonard started with the local flying school. Leonard became a good instrument-rated pilot and obtained his own airplane. He flew all over the country.

"I got to the point where I don't have time for flying," he says. "Right now I'm so preoccupied with a new directing career that I don't have time for anything else. I hope to do both, direct and act. Hard to tell which way it's going to go. There is a lot of new interest in me as a director, so I might find myself very busy directing for a while."

Leonard deliberates over which projects to choose. "I have tried, whenever possible, to work in projects that have some sense of Jewish identity. That's why *A Woman Called Golda* (1981) was a very good experience for me. I went to Israel twice to film it. I played Morris Meyerson, Golda's husband.

"It happened on this Paramount lot. The studio was asking me to work on *Star Trek II: The Wrath of Khan* at the time. As part of the deal, they offered me a role in *A Woman Called Golda.* So I ended up doing both. It worked out very well. I was very pleased with that."

Anti-Semitism has never been a factor in his adult life. As a schoolboy in Boston, he encountered anti-Semitism in the city and in school.

"I used to see anti-Semitic literature. I used to hear people make anti-Semitic remarks. I was very conscious of it.

"There is very little of it in the business here. I have never seen any anti-Semitism in this business, ever. I have never been aware of it. There are a lot of very successful Jewish people in this business. I do not think anti-Semitism would last very long here. I don't think it has a chance to gain a foothold."

Unlike most Jews in Hollywood, Leonard will not work on Rosh Hashanah and Yom Kippur. "Not as a rule, not if I can help it," he insists. His parents now live in Los Angeles and Leonard's family would often join them for the Seder at Passover. Other times they gather for the Seder at the home of his brother Melvin, a chemical engineer. These tend to be large family gatherings, which he enjoys.

To get away from the industry turmoil, the actor goes to his place at Lake Tahoe. "I go there as often as I can. I am involved with very hectic work with a lot of activity and a lot of conversation. I have to get away where it is quiet and peaceful."

Spock (**Leonard Nimoy**) *and Captain Kirk* (**William Shatner**) *in* STAR TREK III: THE SEARCH FOR SPOCK.

Given Name: Leonard Nimoy.
Birthday: March 26, 1931.
Birthplace: Boston, Mass.
Parents: Max and Dora Nimoy.
Sibling: Brother, Melvin, chemical engineer in Los Angeles.
Height: 6′.
Weight: 160 lbs.
Eyes: Brown.
Hair: Dark brown.
Education: Boston English High School; Boston College; Pasadena Playhouse.
Marriage: Sandi Zober (February 21, 1954).
Children: Julie (b. 1955); Adam (b. 1956).
Interests: Photography, poetry, flying.
Personal Habits: Quit smoking 13 years ago.
Clubs: American Civil Liberties Union.
Politics: Democrat.
Social Life: Large family gatherings.
Favorite Book: *Les Miserables* by Victor Hugo
Favorite Movie: *Casablanca.*
Favorite TV Shows: *A Woman Called Golda; Star Trek.*
Career Start: *Pinky Lee Show* on TV (1950).

Profile
Leonard Nimoy

Snack: Celery.
Car: 1973 Mercedes-Benz 280SE.
Pet: Cat.
Ambition: Long vacation.
Vacation Spot: Lake Tahoe.
Charities: Boston Children's Hospital; Venice Family Clinic.
Synagogue: Adat Shalom.
Biggest Mistake: Not going straight to New York when I left home.
Biggest Irritant: Not getting all the facts in a given situation.
Hero: Abraham Lincoln.
Bad Habits: Taking on too much work.
Greatest Achievement: My marriage and my kids.
Kosher: No.
Observe Holidays: Rosh Hashanah, Yom Kippur, Passover Seder.
Jewish Education: Went to Hebrew school from age 8 until bar mitzvah.
Jewish Identity: A very proud identity.
Honors: 4 Emmy nomitations; Sam Beber Award of B'nai B'rith.
Home: Los Angeles.

President Ronald Reagan and Nancy Reagan welcome Freddie Roman to the White House before Freddie's taping of a CBS-TV special at Washington's Ford's Theatre.

*One credo of my life
is that when I work, say at an
Atlantic City hotel, I'm just as
friendly to the bellhops and the
porters as I am to the entertainment directors and the show
people. I like people.*
Quoted in **Ye Epistle**
Friars Club, New York

FREDDIE ROMAN

I watched in astonishment as the Borscht Belt comic was telling the President of the United States what a wonderful country this is. We were at Ford's Theater in Washington, where producer Joe Cates was taping the 1986 *Kraft All-Star Salute to Ford's Theater* for CBS. There were Ronald and Nancy Reagan in the front row, guffawing shamelessly as Freddie Roman related how successive generations ultimately find their way back to their roots.

My grandfather came from Russia in 1906, because he *had* to. He traveled across Europe, crossed the ocean by ship to America, Ellis Island, to a small apartment on Grand Street on the Lower East Side of New York. He worked for sixty years so that he could make a better life for my father. My father lived in Newark, and worked so that I could have a better life, in Jamaica, Queens, where I worked so that I could make a better life for my son. He graduated from college three years ago and said to me, "Daddy, I'm going to Manhattan to live in a small apartment on Grand Street [on the Lower East Side]."

Freddie is a *heimishe mensch*, beloved by all his colleagues in show business. No wonder he was elected entertainment director at the Friars Club in New York.

He is a fine family man who lives in a suburban home with his wife Ethel and a son, Alan, and daughter, Judi. His neighbors in New City, N.Y. are fellow comedians Morty Gunty, Dick Lord, Lenny Rush, and Myron Cohen before he died. "Every Saturday night," Freddie says, "we put on our tuxedos so no one should know who's not working that night."

Congratulate him. He is so proud that after twelve years he has finally paid off the first one hundred dollars on the principal of his mortgage.

A Roman Monologue. . . . . . .

Benefit Dinner for Jerusalem Mental Health Center
Pierre Hotel, New York City, June 16, 1986

My daughter Judi went to England to study. The Queen called for her. She said she's having trouble with Lady Di. You see, she's been a princess for only six years.

My son Alan is twenty-five. I asked him, "What do you want to do?" He says, "I don't know. I want to find myself." I said, "Alan, I know where you are. Okay, I'll give you six months. After that, if you don't find yourself, get lost."

I told President Reagan, don't retire. My parents are retired in Florida, and they fight. My father, a businessman all his life, never went to a meeting. Now he lives in a condo and he goes to a meeting every half hour. I asked why. He said, "They have Danish."

His son Alan, a graduate of the Wharton School of Business at the University of Pennsylvania, is a comedy writer who also trains harness horses at the Meadowlands Race Track in New Jersey. His daughter Judi, a Brandeis graduate, is a law student at Boston University.

Isn't anybody going to follow in daddy's footsteps? Freddie did, at least until it got nauseating. (He should have taken Zero Mostel's advice. When his son Josh opened in an Off-Broadway play, Zero sent him a telegram: "If you want to follow in your father's footsteps, use Desenex.")

He started out in the family trade, selling shoes. His father Harry owned a retail shoe store in Newark where

. . . . . in Honor of Leon Charney

If my mother doesn't change banks every two days, she'd have nothing to do.

I drink L'Chaim, to life. I have a cousin serving L'Chaim in San Quentin.

I'm happy to report I've lost a few pounds. I'm trying to get back to my original weight—seven pounds, four ounces.

At my synagogue, the rabbi said: "People always wonder how long I'll speak. I speak eighteen minutes. That's because it takes me eighteen minutes to walk to the synagogue, and I compose my thoughts on the way. Today I drove from Brooklyn, the traffic was extra heavy . . ."

I'm Jewish, I don't fight—I make settlements. Our wars are over in a week. That's because we use Hertz Rent-a-Tank and we don't want to pay overtime.

Freddie was born in 1937. (When he was two, his family moved to Brooklyn for three years, then relocated to Jamaica, Queens, where he grew up.) His brother George now is men's merchandise manager for the Caldor Department Stores. His other brother Edward is a salesman for an importing firm in the Garment Center.

Freddie tried his hand at selling shoes. He operated his own store in Jamaica. He did well, but dreaded going in every morning. His heart was not in it. He knew he wanted to be a comic. He wanted to make nightclub customers laugh, not shoe customers.

He had been a dramatic arts major at New York University, where his acting partner was a young man named Lou Gossett, Jr. At seventeen, Freddie was an apprentice in summer stock in Hampton, New Hampshire. The next summer he was master of ceremonies at the Biltmore Hotel in Woodridge, New York, for forty dollars a week. The following summer his price as emcee increased to fifty-five dollars at the Homowack Lodge, where he got the opportunity to be bad for forty weeks and hone his craft.

The previous winter he met Ethel at the university where she was studying education (and later became an elementary school teacher). They did not date because he lived in Queens and she in North Bergen, New Jersey. "I didn't want to pay the tolls," he says. His mother would ask, "There are no girls in Queens?"

That summer, Ethel got a job as a counselor at the Almanac Hotel. Freddie was delighted. He said he'd pick her up July 3. That day he brought her to the Homowack. He emceed a show, then drove to Brown's Hotel. It was Jerry Lewis's birthday and Mrs. Brown invited all the comics in the mountains to the party. Freddie joined Phil Foster, Jan Murray, Jack Carter, Dick Shawn and other entertainers working in the various resorts in the Catskills. Each one put on a show until 5:30 in the morning. Then Jerry led everyone out on the lawn and played Simon Sez for an hour.

Still in his tuxedo, Freddie returned to the Homowack at 7:30. He went into the kitchen and helped himself to a cup of coffee. The owner gaped at him and remarked, "I know you're new here. But the social director doesn't have to come to breakfast in a tuxedo. You can wear a pair of shorts."

That was Freddie's first date with Ethel. They married three years later in 1959 at the Park Manor in Brooklyn.

The turning point in Freddie's incipient career came in 1970, at the prestigious Concord Resort in the Catskills. Totie Fields, whom columnist Earl Wilson singled out as "the hottest comedienne in the country," was in the audience. After catching Freddie's show, she ran backstage to tell him how wonderful he was. She did not stop with compliments. She called Juliet Prowse's manager, who was looking for an opening act for her at the Desert Inn in Las Vegas.

She told him, "You're paying him $1500 a week."

He told her, "I only pay $1200."

She insisted, "You'll pay him $1500."

The following month Freddie was working with Prowse in Las Vegas. Totie was in the audience again. She got Freddie more bookings, including one with Steve Lawrence and Eydie Gorme. She even hired him for her show at the Westbury Music Fair in Westbury, N.Y.

"It was most unusual for a comedian to take on another comedian," Freddie marvels. "She never felt threatened."

Totie Fields was a singular human being and Freddie remembers her with love and affection. The raucous-voiced comedy star lost a leg from phlebitis in 1976, and succumbed to a heart attack two years later at age forty-eight.

Freddie readily acknowledges that Totie "opened the doors for me." His show business career started burgeoning. He travels most of the year to the biggest supper clubs in the country and abroad. Wherever he goes, however, he never forgets who he is.

Kings of Comedy Freddie Roman and Alan King upstage the New York **Friars** *as Alan autographs his new book,* **Is Salami and Eggs Better than Sex?**.

Rosh Hashanah and Yom Kippur are inviolable. When he was booked with Tom Jones at Caesars Palace in Las Vegas, the date turned out to be Yom Kippur. Freddie got Jack De Leon to substitute for him that night.

He always enjoys working with Jones, who titillates his female fans to a frenzy. The sexy singer took Freddie on tour. They landed at Mobile, Alabama, where they were met at the airport by a lady limousine driver. They drove and they drove but they were still not anywhere close to the nightclub.

Finally Jones inquired, "Lady, where are you taking us?"

"I'm taking you to my house," she answered.

Freddie was amazed when they pulled up at the chauffeur's house. She had twenty-five women waiting to meet their hip-swinging singing idol.

As for keeping kosher, that is difficult to do on the road. At home, however, *kashrut* is strictly observed. "Ethel is fanatic about it," Freddie says whimsically. "We have twelve closets full of dishes. We have Passover everyday dishes and Passover good dishes."

Their wonderful marriage has endured because Freddie symbolizes the *heimishe mensch*. He is a consummate family man and a paragon in his community. He heads a fund-raising drive every year for his synagogue, the New City Jewish Center. He runs the Freddie Roman Celebrity Golf Tournament to support two local hospitals. He is so apple pie that he is entertaining the thought of running for Congress. I really believe he wants to go back to Washington because he has more jokes for the President.

Freddie's parents live in a retirement community at Sunrise Lake, Florida. Needless to say, they are very happy with their son's career, even though it did not lead to a chain of shoe stores, or to medicine.

"Who did you steal that joke from?" Milton Berle (**third from left**) *asks Henny Youngman* (**right**) *as fellow Friars* (**from left**) *Freddie Roman, Tony Martin, Tom Jones and Red Buttons call out for the cops.*

Given Name: Fred Kirschenbaum.
Birthday: May 28, 1937.
Birthplace: Newark, N.J.
Parents: Harry and Belle Kirschenbaum.
Siblings: Brothers George and Edward.
Height: 5'7".
Weight: 180 lbs.
Eyes: Brown.
Hair: Brown.
Zodiac: Gemini.
Education: Richmond Hill High School, Queens; New York University.
Marriage: Ethel (1959).
Children: Alan, Judi.
Interests: Golf.
Lifestyle: Casual, rural.
Personal Habits: Trying to quit smoking for 35th time; not neat.
Clubs: Friars; Dellwood Country Club.
Politics: Democrat. May run for Congress.
Social Life: Active in the community.
Favorite Book: *The Covenant* by James Michener.

Profile
Freddie Roman

Favorite Movie: *The Frisco Kid* with Gene Wilder.
Snack: Halvah.
Car: Cadillac.
Pets: None.
Ambition: To do a situation comedy on TV.
Exercise: Golf.
Favorite TV Show: *Tonight.*
Charities: UJA; Israel Bonds; New City Jewish Center; run celebrity golf tournament for Nyack and Good Samaritan hospitals.
Hero: Father. I never heard anyone say a bad word about him. That's a nice way to go through life.
Bad Habits: Smoking; procrastination.
Greatest Achievement: My family.
Vacation Spot: La Costa, California.
Kosher: At home.
Holidays: Never work on Rosh Hashanah and Yom Kippur.
Jewish Education: Talmud Torah Mishkan Israel in Jamaica, Queens.
Biggest Regret: As I travel around the world, I see anti-Semitism, even after the Holocaust.
Home: New City, N.Y.

Neil and Leba Sedaka

PHOTO: TIM BOXER

I get an awful lot
of Jewish people in my audience.
They seem to relate to me.
I have that look, that heimish
quality. I think I remind them of
someone in their family.

NEIL SEDAKA

Neil was so busy with piano lessons all through his young years that he almost missed out on his bar mitzvah. The child prodigy was recognized by his second grade teacher, Mrs. Glantz, who told Mrs. Sedaka that her son had tremendous musical talent which should be nurtured. He could some day grow up to be a world-famous concert master. It was very important, the teacher stressed, that the child study piano.

The Sedakas (it used to be Sedacca) lived at 3260 Coney Island Avenue in the Brighton Beach section of Brooklyn. The tiny two-bedroom apartment housed Neil and his sister Ronnie, his parents, his father's parents, and his father's five sisters. Neil's father Mack was born on the Lower East Side, but his parents came from Istanbul. They were Sephardim. Neil's mother Eleanor also was born in Manhattan, but her parents came frm Russia-Poland. They were Ashkenazim. You can say it was a mixed marriage, but a happy one.

His Turkish grandmother made a lasting impression on Neil, who remembers her Sephardic cooking. He listened to all the Sephardic records. He delighted in all the banquets and holidays.

Needless to say, his parents were quite poor. The father was a taxi driver and earned just enough to get by. How in the world could he afford a piano for his son? It was up to Neil's strong-willed mother, who had visions of her son as a brilliant classical musician. She went out to Abraham and Straus department store and got a job as a saleslady. She scraped up enough money, five hundred dollars, to buy a secondhand upright piano.

A private teacher in the neighborhood, Murray Newman, gave Neil piano lessons. After one year, Mr. Newman came to Mrs. Sedaka and told her there was nothing more he could teach her son. Take him to Juilliard. And she did.

Neil was nine years old when he started going to the Juilliard School of Music every Saturday on a scholarship. He went for piano and theory for eight years, until he was graduated from Abraham Lincoln High School.

That is why he almost missed his bar mitzvah. He was so busy with piano lessons and practicing and school work that he had no time for a Hebrew education. He was also music counselor at Rails End Camp in the Pocono Mountains and Echo Lake Camp at Lake George, New Jersey. He would play the piano and compose songs for the kids. To this day people stop Neil on the street and say, "We still sing 'On to the Fray.'"

When her son was already twelve years old, Mrs. Sedaka rushed him to an Ashkenazi synagogue, Temple Beth El, in neighboring Manhattan Beach. At first they refused to take him in, because all the other bar mitzvah candidates had started their studies years earlier.

"My mother went and actually sobbed to the rabbi to take me," Neil says. "She finally succeeded. I did very well. I learned Hebrew. My *haftorah* was so beautiful, there wasn't a dry eye in the congregation on my bar mitzvah morning. The rabbi and cantor went to my mother and said they'd love to make me a *chazan* because I had the most incredible voice. I was a soprano at thirteen. My mother said no, I was going to be a teacher and a pianist."

Nevertheless, Neil loves cantorial music. A lot of his songs reflect that, such as "You Mean Everything to Me" and "Grownup Games." He says he infused a lot of Jewish music into album cuts. He has recorded some twenty-five albums in his songwriting and singing career.

Neil had been writing pop songs since he was thirteen. In high school, he took some of his buddies from math class and formed a singing group, The Tokens. The group went on to record a couple of hits, "Tonight I Fell in Love" and "The Lion Sleeps Tonight."

Still in school, Neil participated in the glee club, the jazz band and the orchestra. He was a very popular music maker. Whenever the movie projector would break down, the kids would chant, "We want Neil. We want Neil." He would get up and play an interlude.

The music teacher, Ben Goldman, submitted Neil's name to the annual WQXR radio classical-music competition. It was open to all high school students, and hundreds auditioned. Neil was among four winners chosen by a panel headed by Arthur Rubinstein to play live on the radio station owned by the *New York Times.*

"I think the thing that clinched it for me," Neil says, "was the last audition when I played Chopin's *G Minor Ballade.* Rubinstein was a great Chopin player. I was so little that my head didn't reach the top of the piano. Rubinstein had to look over the top of the piano to see me. He came up to me and said, 'The Chopin was beautiful, my lad.'"

Neil played for a week on the radio. His teacher listened at home and taped it on a wire recorder. He played it back to Neil, thought it was nice, but then showed him all the things he did not like.

"He was a tough teacher," Neil says. "Now when I listen —I have an old record of it—it's quite good. I played difficult pieces, Prokofiev, Debussy."

After high school Neil got a partial scholarship to Juilliard to continue in the classical world, even though his mind was in the pop sphere. He had written and sold songs to music publishers on Tin Pan Alley. He walked into Atlantic Records where Ahmet Ertegun and Jerry Wexler took his song, but wouldn't take his voice. They thought it was too high-pitched. So Neil wrote the songs that other artists—such as the Cookies, the Cardinals, the Clovers, La Vern Baker, mostly black singers—recorded.

"Strange, for a Jewish boy from Brooklyn," Neil notes. "Yet that ethnic quality, I think, is good. You know, many of us thought of writing R&B music, but we were little Jewish kids from Brooklyn. We listened to black music as kids.

"There's a parallel between Jewish music and the very bluesy black soul music. They are both very lamentful, both in a minor key.

"If you hear a good blues sung by a black person, you know he is black—there are inflections. But if it is sung by another person, it could almost be a Yiddish song—it is sad, it comes from the *kishkes*."

Connie Francis recorded his "Stupid Cupid" and made it gold. He decided to leave Juilliard after eighteen months and concentrate on hit records of his own. He was nineteen.

"My parents at first were very unhappy," he recalls. "Everybody expected Neil to be a concert pianist and teacher. My mother gave me six months to see what I can do."

What Neil did astonished her. He met Don Kirshner, a young Jewish man from the Bronx, who was on the scene hustling as a song plugger, music publisher and artist manager, destined to launch the careers of such stars as Sedaka, Carol King, the Monkees and many others. Kirshner brought Neil to RCA Victor where he recorded

PHOTO: TIM BOXER

Neil Sedaka and George Maharis attend musical revue at Plaza Hotel's PERSIAN ROOM *in Manhattan.*

his first platter as a singer. The ditty was titled "The Diary." When it got air play on radio, Neil's mother would stick her head out of the window on Coney Island Avenue and announce to all of Brooklyn, "My son is singing on the radio!"

The following year, 1959, he followed with two more records, "I Go Ape" and "Oh! Carol." He wrote the latter song as a tribute to a young fan, Carol Klein of Madison High, who used to follow the Tokens around all over Brooklyn. Years later she became super-songwriter Carol King and recorded a tune titled "Oh! Neil," dedicated to her longtime friend.

Neil became one of the most popular pop singers of the sixties, churning out a great number of hit records, among them "Calendar Girl," "Happy Birthday, Sweet Sixteen," "Breaking Up Is Hard to Do." He wrote "Workin' on a Groovy Thing" for the Fifth Dimension, "Don't Hide Your Love" for Cher and "Solitaire" for Andy Williams.

Neil met his wife Leba when he was nineteen and she was sixteen. He had a four-piece band that played at the Esther Manor, a hotel in Monticello in the Catskills. It was run by Irving and Esther Strassberg. Leba was their pretty young daughter. Neil nudged his trumpeter: "See that girl behind the desk? I'm going to marry her." He did, four years later.

"Leba was kosher when I married her," Neil says. "I remember putting a shrimp on her plate. I said, if you can't eat this then you can't travel all over the world with me. She ate it. She thought the heavens would open up. It would have been very difficult being kosher and traveling the way I did."

The English rock invasion in the mid-sixties, spearheaded by the Beatles, shoved Neil Sedaka into the shadows for ten years. It wasn't until Elton John issued a Sedaka album on his own Rocket label that Neil made a comeback. In one year, between 1974 and 1975, he went from making $28,000 to making $5,000,000. That ended the simple life in Brighton Beach. He was now ensconced in an eighteen-room duplex co-op on Park Avenue.

We were sitting in his all-white living room. The carpet is white, the sofa is white, even the grand piano is white. It is a very comfortable home.

"I am sorry there is not more religion in the house," he says now. "But the children know they are Jewish. And I think it is very important to them that they marry within the religion. They are very close to their grandparents. It's a wonderful heritage. Even though they don't observe or worship, if anyone said anything bad, they would absolutely be the first to let him know."

Neil prepares for a day of writing another "hit."

Profile
Neil Sedaka

Given Name: Neil Sedaka.
Birthday: March 13, 1939.
Birthplace: Brooklyn, N.Y.
Parents: Mack and Eleanor Sedaka.
Sibling: Sister, Ronnie, of Fort Lauderdale, Florida.
Height: 5'6".
Weight: 150 lbs.
Eyes: Hazel.
Hair: Dark brown.
Zodiac: Pisces.
Education: Abraham Lincoln High School, Brooklyn; Juilliard School of Music, New York City.
Marriage: Leba Strassberg, 1962.
Children: Daughter, Dara (b. 1963); son, Marc (b. 1966).
Interests: I have my own tennis court in Westport, Connecticut.
Personal Habits: Neatness. I have to hang up everything before I go to sleep.
Social Clubs: None.
Politics: I vote for the person I like.
Social Life: Very active. Being in Manhattan, we go out to two or three parties a night. I have invitations up to here for restaurant openings, people parties, benefits, Meals on Wheels.
First Job: Music counselor at 13 at Camp Echo Lake for $25 for the summer.
Favorite Book: I like a trashy novel by Danielle Steele, which passes the time on a plane.
Favorite Movie: *Blazing Saddles*, which I've seen 20 times.

Neil with wife Leba, son Marc and daughter Dara at SONGWRITERS HALL OF FAME *dinner.*

Snack: Triscuit with Jarlsburg cheese.

Car: Rolls Royce Corniche convertible.

Pets: Fish.

Ambition: I'm starting to play with symphony orchestras and eventually I would like to do a proper concert with pieces in their entirety—Schumann, Brahms, Bartok. Brahms is my favorite. I'm going back to my roots.

Exercise: Bicycle riding in Central Park; daily massage which is like meditation for me.

Charity: Cancer research, diabetes, B'nai B'rith, many others.

Biggest Mistake: I should have performed more in America when I started. The first few years I worked in Europe. That held me back. It took me many years to become known as a performer in the U.S. in the late '50s and early '60s.

Biggest Irritant: Someone who moves slowly. I'm a very fast, spontaneous, impulsive person.

Heroes: George Gershwin, Leonard Bernstein.

Bad Habit: Worrying.

Greatest Achievement: Happy close-knit family. Having achieved notoriety and written songs that have remained timeless.

Vacation Spot: Hawaii, Brazil, Australia.

Kosher: No.

Synagogue: Park Avenue Synagogue, New York City.

Home: Manhattan.

*Abe Vigoda (**right**) and William Hickey (**left**) victimize Tony Roberts in Broadway's classic* ARSENIC AND OLD LACE.

*When I go
to the synagogue today, there is a
deep feeling that this is my
heritage, this is my people. I am
very much moved.
It brings me back to the little boy
who was bar mitzvahed.*

ABE VIGODA

Believe it or not, here is a man who learned his trade in his very first year of school.

"I always suggest to parents," Abe says, "to be careful what they say to children. They do understand and they do remember."

Abe remembers vividly when his first-grade teacher informed the class that she was forming a drama group. The kids would do a play called *Candlelight*. The teacher needed someone to play Baron von Richenhoffen, a fifty-year-old man who finds his wife in the closet with a strange man.

She looked around the room and her eyes settled on a dour child. "You look old, Abe. I think you'll do for the part."

"At six she said I looked old," Abe recalls. "I've been acting ever since."

He has made a career of playing older characters. He has made a concurrent career of gangster types. He scored heavily on Broadway in 1986 in the dramatic comedy, *Arsenic and Old Lace*. The man is adept at his craft which he learned, believe it or not, in the first grade.

Indeed, Abe is so proficient and accomplished an actor that, even though he is often typecast as a heavy, he has performed in many comedic roles. He was a regular on *Four Star Revue* (later changed to *All Star Revue*), a comedy variety show that ran from 1950 to 1953 on NBC. The stars were Jimmy Durante, Ed Wynn, Danny Thomas, George Jessel, Martha Raye, Jack Carson and Tallulah Bankhead. Abe played a variety of comedy roles with the greats of the entertainment industry, including such guest stars as Eddie Cantor and Carmen Miranda. "I started my comedy work there on live television," Abe says.

True to form, while he has played old characters mostly, success came to him late in life. He made his big mark as the Mafia capo Sal Tessio in the 1972 blockbuster motion picture *The Godfather*. As a result of his skillful acting, everyone took him for Italian.

"It was an accomplishment as a performer that they believed I was Italian," Abe says, quite satisfied. "That was really transforming myself from what I am as a person into another human being. That is what we try to do as actors, to go into the skin of another human being."

He attracted phenomenal attention and countless fans with his portrayal of a character this side of the law. His role of Detective Phil Fish on the long-running ABC television series *Barney Miller* (1975-82) is what he is most famous for. He continued his broken-down old cop characterization in his own show on ABC, *Fish* (1977-78).

The actor with the mournful countenance was born on Norfolk Street on the Lower East Side. His immigrant parents came from small towns in Russia. His father was a dressmaker in the Garment Center. The family moved to Brooklyn when Abe was just six years old. Abe attended the Theater School of Dramatic Arts at Carnegie Hall and then the American Theater Wing.

"My life was like a calling to be an actor," he says. "I did not go to the universities, except for a year at Brooklyn College."

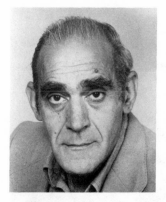

Abe was brought up in an Orthodox home and reads Hebrew fluently. He put on *tefilin* for two years after his bar mitzvah and gave it up. He tries to keep the major holidays as best he can in this business.

"I went out in the world and developed a broader vision," he says. "I involve myself in different charities. I give of myself whether it's for Jew, Catholic, Protestant or black children, as well as such causes as Israel Bonds. Whatever charity I help out, I never forget that deep inside me stirs my Orthodox upbringing."

Married since 1968, Abe met his wife Beatrice, a former accountant, while he was doing a play in San Francisco. He went to a social club to make friends. He was not looking for people in the theater. This discussion group consisted of professionals such as lawyers, engineers and accountants.

He met Beatrice, who had a car. Abe couldn't afford a vehicle. She drove him home. Later she drove him around the city and they became dear friends.

Untl he became affluent with *Barney Miller,* Abe was a struggling actor. He could not afford to play tennis in New York, which meant buying a racquet and renting a court. So he mastered single-wall handball in Central Park and Brighton Beach. "I can actually beat young people in their twenties because of the skill of knowing where to hit the ball," he says proudly.

Profile   Abe Vigoda

Given Name: Abe Vigoda.
Birthday: February 24, 1921.
Birthplace: New York City.
Parents: Samuel and Lena Vigoda.
Sibling: Brother, Hy, retired in Oakland, California.
Height: 6'6".
Weight: 180 lbs.
Eyes: Brown.
Hair: Black.
Zodiac: Pisces.
Education: Brooklyn College (one year); Theater School of
    Dramatic Arts, Carnegie Hall; American Theater
    Wing.
Marriages: Sonja (1949-64); Beatrice (1968).
Children: Daughter, Carol (by Sonja).
Interests: Handball.
Personal Habits: Cigar.
Clubs: Friars.
Charity: Variety Clubs; New York Foundling Home.
Exercise: Jogging.
Favorite TV Show: *60 Minutes.*
Hero: John F. Kennedy.
Bad Habits: Overeating (when I'm frustrated).
Politics: Democrat.
Greatest Achievement: Having been able to maintain my
    health by exercising regularly since I was a young
    boy. It kept me younger and healthier. My doctor told
    me I have the body of a forty-year-old man.
Snack: Sweets. I will nosh when frustrated. This business
    has lots of frustrations.
Vacation Spot: Palm Springs, California.
Social Life: My friends are not necessarily actors. They're
    in other professions, such as engineering, medicine,
    law.
Home: Beverly Hills.

*The Wallace Breed: Sylvia and Irving (**rear**) with their children,
fellow authors David and Amy.*

There was no anti-Semitism
when I was growing up in
Kenosha. There was a Jewishness
among everybody
—Italians, Poles, Lithuanians
—all their families came struggling
out of Europe.

IRVING WALLACE

That explains, perhaps, why Irving Wallace, one of the five most widely-read authors of this century, has never produced a book with a Jewish theme. You might want to count his latest opus as an exception in part. *The Seventh Secret* brings together characters from the United States, Britain and the Soviet Union, plus an Israeli beauty, an agent of Mossad. It is a suspenseful search for Hitler's secret, as yet undiscovered, a survival bunker and the unraveling of an amazing plot to keep the Fuhrer and his mistress alive for years after war's end.

How did the Wallace family end up in the little city of Kenosha, Wisconsin? Bessie Liss came from the Russian town of Narevka, near Bialystock. Ilya Wallechinsky came from Vasilishki, near Vilna. He was a fourteen-year-old lad when he landed on Ellis Island, where an immigration chap promptly tagged him as Alex Wallace. Alex and Bessie met and married in Chicago where Irving was born. A year later they moved to Kenosha, a small town of 50,000 located about fifty miles north of Chicago, where Alex got a job as a clerk in a general merchandise store.

Soon Alex and his younger brother Abe opened their own general store. Although they were not practicing Jews, Bessie kept two sets of dishes ("to look good for other people," Irving says) and Alex went to the Orthodox synagogue rather than the Reform temple ("I suspect because they had a good poker game going there every week").

"I went to *cheder* every day," Irving recalls. "But I was real dumb with languages. I had a terrible time with *alef beis gimel*. I never had a bar mitzvah. I was against it. I didn't want to learn."

A rich uncle consoled Alex: "You don't have to give him a bar mitzvah. He's as Jewish as can be. It will cost a lot of money and you can't afford it, so you don't have to do it."

"So I got off the hook," Irving says.

His mother was very conscious of her Jewishness, even in Kenosha where there were not many Jews. She harbored lingering memories of her childhood in Russia "where there were pogroms and everybody wanted to kill you because of Jesus," Irving says.

His father Alex came from a family of six children. Alex and Ben sent money to enable their sister Sonia to emigrate to the United States. She was very shy and timid. She got a job in town, but after a few years she decided to return to her small town in Poland. Then the war came and the Polish Nazis lined her up with others against the church and shot them down in cold blood.

Irving experienced no anti-Semitic incidents all the time he spent in Kenosha from 1917 to 1935. He ran around with a gang that consisted of an Italian, Pole, German, Lithuanian, Ukrainian and maybe two Jews. Most have moved out to Los Angeles and still see each other.

"There was a Jewishness among everybody—Italians, Poles, Lithuanians. All their families came struggling out of Europe. Their families were old-country religious. But none of us were religious in the sense of practicing. We read philosophy. We were liberated people, getting away from the old-fashioned ways. Religion was never an issue.

"My wife never believed me when I told her there was no anti-Semitism in Kenosha. She suffered a lot of it in the Bronx in those days. She grew up among Irish cops and pseudo-Nazis. She's very Gentile-looking so they would talk in front of her. She has memories.

"One day I got a book by Ben Hecht who came from Racine, ten minutes from Kenosha. He wrote that he never knew anti-Semitism until he left Racine. Then she believed me."

Irving had no familiarity with anti-Semitism until 1935, when he got a scholarship to Williams Institute in Berkeley, California. He was elated at the offer because it was a writer's school with a visiting faculty that boasted such names as William Saroyan, Lincoln Steffens and Rupert Hughes.

"One of the guys I loved the most shocked me," Irving related. "We went to a bar on Saturday night and he began talking against Jews. He didn't know I was a Jew. So I looked at him. That was my first consciousness that in some way I was separate. I told him. He said he was very embarrassed. He said he didn't mean it and that I was a special person."

After two terms, Irving left the school. What good was it? They were teaching how to write for magazines and Irving had already published close to a hundred articles. He started writing at thirteen and sold his first piece two years later for five dollars. He was editor of the high school paper and won national writing contests.

"Writing, that's all I ever knew," he says. "I was good; childish, but good. The big magazines in those days were the *Saturday Evening Post, Reader's Digest* and *Collier's.* I sold to them when I was older."

Irving headed south for the Hollywood hills and wrote magazine articles until he enlisted in the Army in 1942. A cavalry officer named Ronald Reagan signed him up for the First Motion Picture Unit of the Army Air Force in Culver City, where they made training films. In 1944 he transferred to the Army Signal Corps Photographic Center in Los Angeles and worked on two dozen orientation films, with directors John Huston and Frank Capra and script-writer Carl Foreman.

Colonel Capra's outfit was making a film titled *Know Your Enemy Japan*. "He was quite an impossible man despite his great reputation," Irving says.

They couldn't elicit a policy from Washington on how to treat the Japanese in the film. Are the Japanese all bad? Is the military all bad? Is the Emperor bad?

Capra growled, "I'll give you a policy—the only good Jap is a dead Jap."

"We said that was racist," says Irving. "We didn't say that to him because he was our boss. We said it to each other. The only good Jap is a dead Jap. The only good Indian is a dead Indian. The only good Jew is a dead Jew."

They begged Capra to bring some experts in from Washington to discuss policy. He did, and a policy finally evolved, thanks to Wallace and Foreman. The policy: The Japanese military was responsible. A lot of people were responsible, but we can't bury the whole Japanese nation. Leave the Emperor alone, because we need a figurehead.

After the war, with filmwriting experience in the service, Irving got a screenwriting job at Warner Brothers for $750 a week.

He hated it. Irving is basically a loner, a one-man factory churning out hundreds of magazine articles in his early years and thirty-three popular books to date (most of them best-sellers, several in conjunction with his family).

Not only did this freedom-loving soul acquire a boss (Jack Warner) but collaborators as well. It was group writing. That is the nature of scriptwriting. You are dependent on director and actress. "Irving, I can't read these lines," Doris Day would murmur. "Why don't we do something like this." And she would scribble her own stuff.

"I've never known of a group effort that accomplished anything, except one—the King James Bible. It was the only successful collaboration by more than two people."

In recent years Irving collaborated with his wife and children on such books as *Intimate Sex Lives of Famous People* and *Book of Lists.*

His first big picture was for James Cagney. Irving was inspired by an incident with columnist Westbrook Pegler. Because he was always making fun of West Point, Pegler was invited to become a cadet for a day, to see if he could take it. After that he never picked on the academy again.

Irving thought to himself: "Hey, what if there's a wise guy, Cagney, who they want to get to West Point to direct their musical. But he says, 'Oh, those bums, who cares? I'm big time!' I got the idea from Pegler. *West Point Story* came out in 1950, co-starring Doris Day. It was nominated for the Writers Guild Award. It did well, but it wasn't a superb picture. It was a group effort."

Did Cagney change any lines from Irving's script?

"He did more than that," Irving reveals. "I finished the script myself. Then, since I wasn't experienced enough, this being my first picture, they gave me a rather nice guy to collaborate with on a new draft. They approved it. But Cagney said he wanted to bring in his own writer. So they re-wrote it once more."

Warner Brothers paid $100,000 for a best-seller, *Too Much, Too Soon* (1958) and brought the author Gerold Frank out to Hollywood to do the screenplay. They told him that since he had no experience in scriptwriting, he would work with Wallace.

"It didn't work out very well," Irving says, again confirming that too many cooks spoil the broth.

"We were dear friends but it was awfully hard to collaborate with somebody. He wanted everything his way, like he wrote in the book. I knew more about movies by then, and I knew a script can't be like the book. You have to change it."

Irving left Hollywood to the professional team-writers and returned to the lonely task of turning out best-selling novels.

"I never thought you could get rich on books. But I knew books—nobody would interfere with me. Nobody."

He wrote four books and couldn't make a living at it. In 1960 came *The Chapman Report* and it was a worldwide hit. The movie in 1962 starred Jane Fonda.

"That book made me independent," says Irving. "I quit everything. I wouldn't go near magazines, movies, anything, because it made a lot of money. The next book I wrote, *The Prize* in 1962, was even bigger."

Now he makes a very good living, especially from those many books that are turned into major motion pictures. He is one of the most widely read authors in the world. *Newsweek* reported that the biggest selling author is Harold Robbins, second is Irving Wallace and third is Louis L'Amour. In 1985, Irving Wallace points out, 52,000 books were published in the United States. He thinks only a hundred people are making a living on books, without resorting to side money from teaching, lecturing, magazine writing or rich wives.

"The average book sells three thousand to five thousand copies," he says. "A best-seller sells one hundred thousand hardback, maybe two million more paperback, just in this country. So you can make money in books. I sold everything to the movies, and that was just extra money."

His success is reflected in his lifestyle. His sprawling home—actually two separate houses linked together—consists of seventeen comfortable rooms. The double house, valued at two million dollars, is located in the exclusive Brentwood section of Los Angeles. It is secluded from the street by a neatly trimmed hedgerow. The driveway holds two cars belonging to his secretaries. Step inside the door at the right and you find yourself in an office, with desks, telephones, copying machines, and one room completely filled with rows of filing cabinets. They are filled with a lifetime of personal papers, correspondence, rejection slips from the very early days of magazine writing, and a horde of items and facts useful for future writing.

A secretary opened a huge, brown wooden door and I stepped into a cavernous beamed room. Irving strutted across the floor, emitting clouds of gray smoke from the pipe in his mouth, as he welcomed me to his literary quarters. The walls were covered with books from floor to high ceiling.

His personal interests are evident. Near the door is a red chair that once belonged to Lewis Carroll at Oxford, which Irving acquired at auction. He collects artifacts and antiques, some of which are displayed in museum-type glass cases. Another red chair belonged to Charles Dickens. He has Charles Dickens' traveling desk, which Dickens used while traveling by stagecoach. He also has Conan Doyle's traveling desk which he used on the train.

One entire wall consists of rare books signed by the authors. There is a complete set of Somerset Maugham's books, signed. He has the first edition, signed copies of D. H. Lawrence's *Lady Chatterly's Lover* and Dashiel Hammett's *The Thin Man*.

"I love Tolstoy, Stendhal and Dickens," he says. "Among modern writers, I love Maugham for his clarity, style, cynicism, and wit. I got them all, not his plays, just his novels and non-fiction."

His huge wooden writing desk is cluttered with gadgets from around the world. Whenever anybody from the family travels, they bring back some chachkeh for his kitsch collection.

"I got the idea from Roosevelt. As a kid I admired Franklin Delano Roosevelt. Whenever I saw a picture of his desk, it always had all kinds of little things. So I began putting them there. Friends bring them to me. Now my grandchildren play with them, break them."

Next to his desk is his prize typewriter. His parents gifted him with the Underwood on his thirteenth birthday. They did not have much money, so they bought a rebuilt model. He thinks it was made in 1914. It has been rebuilt many times since then. His son David uses an IBM computer.

David is the co-author (with Michael Medved) of *What Really Happened to the Class of '65* and sole author of the sequel, *The Midterm Report: The Class of '65.* He lives in Santa Monica with his wife Flora Chavez, who is part American Indian and part Chicano.

Before Irving's father died five years ago, he was having dinner with the entire family when he told the story of how his name was changed on Ellis Island. David Wallace was incensed. So when he sold his book, he adopted the original family name and became David Wallechinsky.

I was impressed with David's decision to carry on the family name but why, I asked, did he abandon the family faith? David and his sister Amy Wallace had told me several years ago that they had joined the Church of the Divine Men. "Yes," Amy laughed. "It's been called a sexist church."

"No, not true," Irving declares. "He's quite good about Jewish stuff. He has two sons now, Elijah and Aaron. He learned a lot of Yiddish when we were in Miami Beach for the Republican and Democratic conventions. He stayed at a home for elderly people. They were all Jewish, they spoke Yiddish, and he picked up the language very fast. He is very Jewish, but doesn't go to temple."

"David said he is a minister in the church," I continue.

"Oh, that," Irving says. "I am too, and so is Amy. For a dollar in California you can send to a certain church and you may perform weddings. We did it for fun. I have it on my wall. It's not a practicing church. It's a mail-order thing.

"David did not convert to Christianity. Never. That was just a gag, for fun. He is Jewish and married to a fallen-off Catholic, a Hispanic girl, a very beautiful airline stewardess. He is very interested in his Jewish background."

Profile
Irving Wallace

Given Name: Irving Wallace.
Birthday: March 19, 1916.
Birthplace: Chicago, Illinois.
Parents: Alex Wallace and Bessie Liss.
Sibling: Sister, Esther Biederman, of Tarzana, California.
Height: 5'10".
Weight: 168 lbs.
Eyes: Brown.
Hair: Gray.
Marriage: Sylvia Kahn (1941).
Children: David (b. 1948), Amy (b. 1955).
Education: Kenosha High School, Kenosha, Wisconsin.
Interests: First-edition signed books, artifacts, gadgets, paintings (Picasso, Chagall, Modigliani, Matisse).
Lifestyle: Travel a lot, always first class, stay in suites, not rooms.
Personal Habits: Pipe smoker, social drinker, poker player.

Clubs: PEN, Authors League of America (Writers Guild).

Politics: Democrat.

First Job: A year after high school, the labor union in Kenosha hired me at starvation wages, maybe $15 a week, to produce a paper, *The South Port Bugle*. I was the whole staff.

Favorite Books: *Of Human Bondage* by Somerset Maugham; Stendhal's *The Red and the Black*, Dickens' everything.

Favorite Movies: *One Flew Over the Cuckoo's Nest, It Happened One Night.*

Snack: American cheese sandwich on diet toast; crackers with butter; candy.

Pet: Cat.

Ambition: I would just like to write better. I want to exist as a writer. I don't want to be past tense.

Home: Brentwood, California.

"Take my wife, please" Henny with wife, Sadie.

*I like to work
in New York better than California
—you get paid
three hours earlier.*

HENNY YOUNGMAN

"Call me Sunday and we'll have brunch," Henny Young-man said.

I called him, and true to his word we had brunch... on the phone. He had bagels and lox at the Carnegie Delicatessen and I had a cheese omelette at home.

He told me he was going on Johnny Carson's *Tonight Show* on NBC. "I'll be on with Dolly Parton. If you can keep your eyes off her voice, look for me." He will discover that Dolly can make any line in the dialogue as exciting as her neckline. Henny, no slouch at chitchat, will offer such gems as this one:

> I met Frank Sinatra at the 21 Club. He said, "What are you doing here?" I said, "I don't usually eat here. I eat next door, at 20."

After cracking up on the phone, I met Henny at his favorite hangout. Leo Steiner, proprietor of the Carnegie Deli and pastrami potentate of Seventh Avenue, ushered me to the table where the King of the One-Liners (because he can't remember two) was holding court with an audience of guffawing waiters and customers.

I just came back from a pleasure trip—I drove my mother-in-law to the airport...I found out how to solve the traffic problem—I bought a parked car... My mother-in-law is in the Olympics—she's a javelin catcher.

He called a waiter, "Statue!" He came over and the comedian said, "When you get a chance, come back."

He wore a belt with a double G buckle, very chic. "Stands for guts," he remarks. "You need guts to tell these jokes."

Like the time he visited a synagogue in Beverly Hills—B'nai Gucci.

The waiters were chuckling and chortling. "It's so noisy here I can't hear myself think," I said.

"You're lucky," Henny shot back.

Finally, Henny ordered from the waiter: "Give me burned toast, soggy eggs, cold coffee."

"We don't serve that here."

"You did yesterday."

Don't try to top the man the *New York Times* called "the world-class master of the carefully constructed one-liner." He will only demolish you. Like the time Red Buttons attacked: "Henny, where are you going in this business?" And Henny shot back, "To the bank."

No, you have no chance of topping the king...unless you're a brash young hustler with the gift of con. It happened to him on Broadway, where a young flower peddler, not more than twelve years old, stopped Henny in his tracks with this spiel: "Mister, would you buy a flower if I tell you your first name, your last name, the state you were born in, how many children you got, how many birthdays you had, and where you got your clothes?"

Intrigued, since even he did not know all the answers, Henny relented. "Your first name," the kid went on, "was baby, your last name will be corpse, you were born in the state of infancy, you didn't have children—your wife had them, you only had one birthday, the rest were anniversaries, and you got your clothes on." Henny walked away with a stale gardenia and a billfold minus a dollar.

Henny's parents came from Russia, married in New York and honeymooned in London. They tarried there for a year and Henny was born in Whitechapel in the East End. They moved back six months later and settled in the Bay Ridge section of Brooklyn. His father Jack was a window dresser at Kresge's five-and-dime store in downtown Brooklyn.

Henny went to Manual Training High School, but he was more interested in cutting up than buckling down. He was the class clown and was thrown out on more than one occasion. His teacher would put him in the detention room, where he was expected to sit silently for two hours. He didn't sit. He would sneak out to the four neighborhood vaudeville theaters (Orpheum, Prospect, Flatbush, Fox) for those two hours. For fifteen cents admission, he would absorb a tremendous number of jokes from the comedians on stage. He memorized the funny lines and became the life of any party he went to.

As a child, he had been forced to take violin lessons. "I played two ways—for pleasure or revenge," he says. "I played a concert and people shouted, 'Less! Less!'" He got such laughs with his fiddling that he gave up trying to be a musician and became a comedian with a fiddle. As he told Buttons, he's been going to the bank ever since.

His father wanted him to learn a trade, so he sent him to Brooklyn Vocational Trade School. He went into the printing business, with a concession at Kresge's. He printed business cards while-you-wait. That's where he met his wife, Sadie, who worked at the cosmetics counter.

He started out with a combo, but his meager musicianship was quickly overshadowed by his mirth-provoking wisecracks. It first happened at a little night spot in Mountainside, New Jersey, the Nut Club. One night, the dance team of Grace and Paul Hartman did not show up. (Their son is David Hartman, former host of ABC's *Good Morn-*

King Of The One-Liners

★ A psychiatrist is a Jewish doctor who can't stand   the sight of blood.

★ He thinks High Cholesterol is a Jewish holiday.

★ Israeli Navy slogan: Don't give up the ship—sell it.

★ One Jewish lady says to the other, "Do you see what's going on in Lebanon?" The other says, "I don't see anything. I live in the back of the building."

★ Won't last long—they're as compatible as ham and matzah.

★ I wanted to become an atheist but I gave it up. They have no holidays.

★ My wife had a fight with her mother so she's coming home.

★ One word you never hear in my house is divorce. Murder, yes, but divorce, no.

★ When I go to Israel, in Milton Berle's honor I will have a tree uprooted.

★ What do you call a Jewish baby who isn't circumcised? A girl.

ing America.). Henny reached into his storehouse of jokes memorized from those vaudeville theaters he frequented when he should have been sitting in school, and went on instead. He was a riot and a comedy king was born.

Still a teenager, he got his first job in vaudeville on Rosh Hashanah. With fiddle in hand, he would make the rounds of the agents looking for bookings. One day, Jack and Mark Linder, who handled Mae West, offered him a job at the Sixteenth Street Theater in Brooklyn. It paid three dollars. They neglected to tell him that it was on Rosh Hashanah. When the day came, he went. The theater was near Temple B'nai Israel, where Henny had gone to *cheder* and where he was supposed to be that day for services with his dad. Right in the middle of his act, his father and a police officer marched up the aisle and dragged him off the stage. He never got the three dollars.

He knocked around the speakeasies and cellar clubs before hitting it off at the Yacht Club on West Fifty-second Street. It was a rowdy era of gangsters and entertainers. One night a guy came into his dressing room and asked to borrow a shirt. He said he had spilled wine on his. "I gave him one of my shirts," Henny said, "but when he saw my monogram he wouldn't take it. Next day I learned he'd stabbed someone and the police had traced him by a bloody shirt. I was relieved he hadn't taken my shirt."

Henny worked at the Club Kennedy. It used to be known as the Club Abbey, but when a hood was knocked off there, it had a change of name. He would begin his monologue by telling the roughnecks, "I wasn't sure they'd let me in here—I don't have a police record." That loosened them up and Henny was off and running.

Another joint he worked was the Showplace on Long Island. Every night one of the regulars would drive him home to Manhattan. Henny did not know it at the time, but the nice fellow turned out to be a petty hood named Pretty Amberg who, when aroused, delighted in gouging a hole in your cheek with a broken glass. He ended up in a cement suit.

Henny achieved national recognition when he was on the *Kate Smith Show* on radio for two years, starting in 1936. He had seven of the best writers grinding out one-liners. "All these other guys used to take my jokes down and then go into the business. They didn't have any money to buy jokes. I started forty comedians in the business— Jan Murray, Buddy Hackett, Red Buttons." Some of his best lines:

* My uncle was psychic. Knew exactly the day he'd die—the warden told him.

* I had a terrible accident on the way to the track— I got there safely.

* My mother was eighty-eight years old. Never needed glasses—drank right out of the bottle.

His wife came to watch the show and brought a group of friends. Henny told the usher, "Take my wife, please," and the audience broke up. He meant that the usher should escort her to a seat. He has used that line ever since, to great effect. It has become his signature, like Rodney Dangerfield's "I get no respect," and Red Buttons' "Strange things are happening."

The highlight of his Jewish life came when he entered adulthood...at age seventy-three. According to time-honored custom, a Jewish boy comes of legal age at thirteen when he is inducted into the House of Israel through a bar mitzvah ceremony, which includes intoning the blessings as a portion of the Torah is read—in the original Hebrew. Henny's bar mitzvah had been canceled when a cousin died. It was never rescheduled because the family was poor. So Henny never solemnized his rite of passage to adulthood. When he was booked at Resorts International in Atlantic City in 1980, the entertainment director found out from a local newspaperman that Henny had never had a bar mitzvah and decided the time had come. He arranged the whole thing on Saturday morning, the day of Henny's opening in the nightclub, in a ballroom that was turned into a temple.

Henny did not know a word of Hebrew. He turned to a longtime friend, Leonard Goldstein, president of Centre City Corporation. A graduate of Yeshiva University who became a pharmacist, Leonard operates drugstores and gift shops in a string of hotels, including the New York Hilton and the St. Regis. He met with Henny at Hurlingham's Bar at the Hilton and they rehearsed phonetic pronunciatons of the Hebrew blessings over the Torah. Two such classes and several stiff drinks later, Henny was ready for his *aliyah*, to be called up to the Torah.

Nobody ever had such a bar mitzvah in the history of the Jewish people, and I doubt if it will be repeated. Jan Peerce agreed to serve as cantor, and Rabbi Seymour Rosen of Margate, New Jersey, conducted the hour-long Reform service. He was sixty years late, but Henny could not have been more proud to finally become a man, or as he put it, "Today I am a boy."

A battery of television cameras and still photographers lined the entire breadth of the back of the room where three hundred and fifty guests, including reporters, were seated. Jack Kelly, brother of Princess Grace of Monaco, came from Philadelphia to add social significance to the momentous event. Leo Steiner represented Salami Society. Norm Crosby came from Caesars Boardwalk Regency down the street. Of course, Henny's wife Sadie trekked up from her winter home in Miami, accompanied by their son Gary, and daughter Marilyn Kelly and her son Larry.

When the rabbi turned to Henny and said, "Take this Bible—please," the bar mitzvah boy knew it was time to deliver his speech. It was written by Carroll Carroll, a columnist on *Variety*, the show business bible.

It was a speech full of humor and pathos. "I'm being bar mitzvahed now," Henny reflected, "because it took me fifty years to memorize the speech." One of the many telegrams read: "Congratulations on your bar mitzvah at seventy-three. Lucky it wasn't your bris!"

Henny saws away at a "fiddle" for a laugh.

A Bar Mitzvah Speech

After fifty years in show business, it seemed that no matter what I did somebody would say Johnny Carson did that, or Bob Hope did that. Well, let them try THIS!

Bar mitzvahs for grownups could bring back the old-fashioned fountain pen. The kind that leaked in your pocket. I've gotten sixty-three. One was real gold, one was real silver, and one had real ink. And they were all engraved with a little wish after the name: Ronald Reagan—vote for me.

People keep asking me—at your age, why bar mitzvah? I wanted to settle forever the endless arguments over whether or not I'm Jewish. But that was just a toss-up. The Gentiles and the Jews flipped a coin. The Jews lost. So they held a circumcision. That was the unkindest cut of all.

Of course, as I stand here I think of my dear mother and father. How I wish they could be here— my mother crying with a heart full of joy, my father crying with a handful of bills. How proud they'd be of my standing here in my blue suit, with my hair combed.

It's been a long wait. All my bar mitzvah arrangements were made back when I was thirteen. But it had to be postponed. The caterers went out on strike. So my agent started booking club dates. This is the first free day I've had in sixty years. How time flies. It really made me feel bad to miss that bar mitzvah. I had to send back all the presents.

I'm grateful to Resorts International for arranging all this. It sort of makes them my parents. At last I got rich ones.

Given Name: Henry Youngman.
Birthday: March 16, 1906.
Birthplace: London, England.
Parents: Yonkel (Jack) Yungman and Olga Chetkin.
Sibling: Brother, Lester, novelty salesman (deceased).
Height: 6'2".
Weight: 225 lbs.
Eyes: Lovely green eyes.
Hair: Was blond, now dyed.
Zodiac: Pisces.
Education: Manual Training High School; Brooklyn Vocational Trade School.
Marriage: Sadie Cohen (May 4, 1928).
Children: Son, Gary, film editor; daughter, Marilyn Kelly, housewife.
Interests: Looking for new comedians to help and give them jokes.
Clubs: Friars.
Politics: Vote for each guy once.
Social Life: People from all over the world come to visit me, and I take them to dinner at the Carnegie Deli, Italian Pavilion or the Friars Club.
Favorite Book: Joke books.

Profile
Henny Youngman

Favorite Movie: *History of the World: Part I.*
Snack: Piece of chicken.
Car: Not in New York. If I get a job, they have to send for me in a limousine.
Pet: My grandson Jamie.
Ambition: To star in a picture, like Rodney Dangerfield.
Exercise: Getting up in the morning.
Charity: Little City Foundation in Palatine, Illinois; helping retarded people.
Hero: Milton Berle.
Bad Habits: Eating too much.
Greatest Achievement: Doing *Kate Smith Show* for two years.
Vacation: My home in Woodstock, New York.
Biggest Regret: Not saving more money. I invested where I shouldn't have. I would be much richer today if I wasn't in the stock market.
Jewish Identity: Everybody knows I'm Jewish—I let them know.
Kosher: No.
Observe Holidays: Yom Kippur.
Synagogue: Actors Temple, New York City.
Home: 77 West 55th Street, New York, N.Y. 10019.

JEWISH
CELEBRITIES
HALL OF FAME
PICTURE PARADE

LAUREN BACALL

Betty Jane Perske was born September 16, 1924, in Greenwich Village, New York. She co-starred with husband Humphrey Bogart in **To Have and Have Not** *and* **The Big Sleep**. *She earned a Tony for* **Applause** *and* **Woman of the Year**. *She neatly summed up her Jewish connection with these words in her autobiography,* **Lauren Bacall By Myself**: *"Going back through my life now, the Jewish family feeling stands proud and strong, and at least I can say I am glad I sprang from that. I would not trade those roots — that identity."*

Burt and mother, Irma.

BLANCHE BAKER

Emmy-winning actress of NBC's **Holocaust** *miniseries was born December 20, 1956. She starred on Broadway in* **Lolita** *but unlike her mom, Carroll Baker, who created a sensation as a screen siren in* **Baby Doll***, Blanche resists the sex symbol stereotype—she also portrayed the Virgin Mary on television in* **Joseph and Mary***. Her mother converted to Judaism when she married director Jack Garfein, a survivor of nine concentration camps who weighed 48 pounds at age 14 when he was liberated from Bergen-Belsen. Blanche did not allow her father's experience and the annihilation of his entire family to embitter her heart. 'Don't let it cut you off from life. What I got from the Jewish religion is an appreciation of life...As a Jew, I still have to have faith in the universe and in mankind.'*

BURT BACHARACH

The composer of "Raindrops Keep Fallin' On My Head" and "Walk on By" was born May 12, 1929, in Kansas City, Missouri, and raised in Kew Gardens, Queens. His father was fashion columnist Bert Bacharach. Formerly married to Paula Stewart and Angie Dickinson, he now is hitched to songwriter-partner Carole Bayer Sager and lives in Bel Air, California.

POLLY BERGEN

"I'm probably the only Jewish Southern Baptist in the United States," says the actress-business executive who was born July 4, 1930, in Knoxville, Tennessee, as Nellie Pauline Burgin, granddaughter of a Baptist minister. She converted after she married agent Freddie Fields (whom she divorced and is now married to Jeff Endervelt). She says it was strictly her decision to convert to Judaism because *"the more I was exposed to Freddie's faith, the more I was convinced that it was a religion that made sense to me."*

MICHAEL BRANDON

The Brooklyn-born actor lived with Kim Novak for a while, then married Lindsay Wagner, TV's **Bionic Woman***. Now he is in England starring in* **Dempsey and Makepeace***, cop series, shown in syndication in the U.S. When he first went to California in the early '70s, his mother, Miriam Feldman, would write to Johnny Carson to put him on* **The Tonight Show** *so she could see if he was eating right. It worked.*

JAY BERNSTEIN

Hollywood's supreme starmaker was born June 7, 1937, in Oklahoma City. As a personal manager he created the images of several leading ladies of television series. As Dr. Joyce Brothers lovingly put it at a roast in his honor: 'Jay became Farrah Fawcett's manager and she fired him. He became Suzanne Somers' manager and she fired him. I guess you can say he's the best all-fired manager around.' His latest project is producing the **mike hammer** *series on CBS.*

Jay and Linda Evans.

JON BAUMAN

Sha Na Na's inimitable Bowzer hails from the Williamsburgh section of Brooklyn and grew up in Queens. A product of the '50s, Jon was a child prodigy at the piano, started classical lessons at seven, and entered Juiliard at twelve. He joined the group as pianist and vocalist while they were Columbia University students, and reached their height during the '70s on their syndicated television show. "I created the first re-definition of the 50s character," he says. *"Later came* **Grease** *and Fonzie."*

CLAIRE BARRY

The famed Barry Sisters passed into history with the untimely death of older sister Myrna in 1976. Claire began an uphill battle to make a comeback as a solo singer with new material. When Ed Sullivan brought the duo to the Soviet Union in the first cultural exchange in 1960, Claire found that the Russians were getting the Barry sisters albums underground. "After we left, the Russian papers reported that we were killed in a plane crash. Now whenever I do concerts, Russian immigrants in America are amazed to see me again."

Paula and Dick.

RICHARD BENJAMIN

*The actor was born May 22, 1939, in New York. Married to non-Jewish actress Paula Prentiss. He starred in two Philip Roth stories, **Goodbye Columbus** (1968) and **Portnoy's Complaint** (1972). He has since become a much sought-after film director.*

SHERRY BRITTON

*A strip teaser since she was thirteen, Sherry was very popular with both sides in World War II. An American soldier sent her a photo of herself in an ostrich covered frame which he had lifted from a dead German soldier in 1944. "If the German had known he was carrying around a picture of a Jewish girl," Sherry says, "he wouldn't have had to be killed. He would have committed suicide." Sherry was born Edith Britton in 1924, in New Brunswick, New Jersey. Her father was violinist Charles Britton of Dublin; her mother was Esther Dansky of Grodno Gubernia on the Russian-Polish border. Throughout her exotic career, most people did not know Sherry was Jewish. In fact Larry Adler refused to hire her for the play **A Flag is Born**, in 1946. "He hired Marlon Brando as a narrator but turned me down because I didn't look Jewish," she recalls. Nevertheless, she declares, "I always had a Jewish heart because I was always proud of my heritage.*

DYAN CANNON

Samille Diane Friesen was born January 4, 1937, in Tacoma, Washington, to a Jewish mother, Clara Portnoy, and non-Jewish father, Ben Friesen, a rancher. She was married to Cary Grant, 1956-68, and bore him his only child, Jennifer. Grant had been married five times. Dyan was Oscar-nominated for **Bob & Carol & Ted & Alice**, **Heaven Can Wait**, *and* **Number One***.*

SAMMY DAVIS

America's one-eyed Jewish Negro — as Sammy Davis Jr. has described himself — is this country's consummate entertainer. He is Mr. Everything — from singer, dancer, actor, mimic, comedian to author, producer and director.

He's also a man who is proud to be a Jewish convert.

He brought his act to the Concord Hotel in the Borscht Belt, where a woman stopped him on the golf course.

"Are you really Sammy Davis?" she inquired.

*"With this **punim** who else could I be?" he retorted.*

"I wasn't sure it was you," she rejoined, adding, "You don't have your jewelry on."

Attorney Leon Charney, who represents the Concord among other prestigious clients, reminded Sammy of the two times they both went to Israel. Sammy recalled the thrill of entertaining the troops right after the Six Day War in 1967.

He was also there for Jewry at a prayer service in West Hartford, Connecticut, after arsonists torched a Young Israel Synagogue.

"When I saw the destruction that the fire did to your synagogue," he told the congregants, "my Jewish heart wept as all of us are now weeping." He added that Jews must respond to such attacks by bigots by meeting the challenge "as one people united in their determination that our spirit is still strong and vibrant."

The black entertainer, who converted thirty years ago, said that when he accepted Judaism it was because "I wanted to be part of that strong and steadfast tradition that withstood and overcame thousands of years of bigotry and persecution."

Sammy, born December 8, 1925, in New York City, was brought up in the Catholic faith, although his was not a churchgoing family. His mother, the former Elvera Sanchez, is Catholic; his father is Baptist.

When Sammy appeared on the **Eddie Cantor Comedy Theatre** television show he admired a mezuzah in the host's dressing room. Cantor gave it to him, and Sammy has worn it on his neck ever since — save for one day. That was in 1954, the year he lost an eye in an auto accident. Cantor visited him in the hospital and inquired about the mezuzah. With a crestfallen expression on his face, Sammy said that the day of the accident was the first that he had not put on the mezuzah — he had misplaced it.

He thought about these two incidents while convalescing in a hospital in San Bernardino. They caused him to reflect on his faith — such as it was. He talked it over with a Jewish chaplain, and when he left the hospital he took with him several books that had been recommended. Out of the hospital, he continued conversations with rabbis andslowly, over the course of many months, came to a point when he was ready to make a commitment. He would convert.

His parents supported his decision, but his Jewish friends did not. They attempted to dissuade him because they feared the public would take the conversion as a publicity stunt.

Sammy, accompanied by Leon Charney, is welcomed to Israel by El Al and army officials on his way to entertain fellow Jewish troops after Six Day War.

PHOTO: ISRAEL SUN

PHOTO:TIM BOXER

David C. Gross' **The Jewish People's Almanac** *quotes Sammy on why he chose Judaism: "I found something here that gave me a feeling of refreshing simplicity. It was an understanding of life all around me. I wanted to become a Jew because the customs of Judaism hold a cleanliness that no other philosophy on this earth can offer. I'm a Jew and proud of it."*

Shortly after he converted, Sammy was filming **Porgy and Bess** *near Stockton, California. He told the director he wouldn't work on Yom Kippur. The man turned pale and called Sam Goldwyn in Hollywood. The feared movie mogul called Sammy right back. "What's this I hear, Sammy? You won't be on the set tomorrow?"*

Sammy explained that as a Jew he would not work on Yom Kippur. There was silence, then Goldwyn mumbled "Bless you" into the telephone and hung up. Production was held up for that one day — at a cost of $30,000.

At the Concord, I asked Sammy if he regretted changing his faith. "Absolutely not," he replied. "It's been a constant source of reassurance. I chose it because it gave me answers, spiritual answers, that I needed.

"What does it mean to be a Jew? Very simple. It's part being a good human being, part realizing there is a commitment to the heritage which either you are born into or are allowed to adopt. Those are the responsibilities — and heavy duties — and you have to live up to them."

JULES FEIFFER

A social satirist, cartoonist Jules Feiffer was born January 26, 1929, in New York. He calls himself a cultural Jew; otherwise he's been an atheist since shortly after his bar mitzvah. "I'm not an idolatrous atheist," he says. "I associate myself with that tradition of European socialist/atheist/anarchist." His incisive social and political commentaries in his strip in the **Village Voice** *(since 1956) and other papers have a wide loyal following. He has also written plays and novels. His hobbies include television, reading and hiding out in bed. From whom? "From them—Ronald Reagan and the theatre critics," says the Pulitzer Prize-winning cartoonist.*

Kirk Douglas

Born Issur Danielovich Demsky on December 9, 1916, in Amsterdam, New York, and raised in poverty by a Russian immigrant junk dealer, Kirk climbed to the heights of cinematic stardom through seventy motion pictures and three Academy Award nominations. His films include **A Letter to Three Wives**, **Champion**, **The Juggler**, **Paths of Glory**, **The Vikings**, **Spartacus**, and **Cast a Giant Shadow**. M. Kaplan, a Bronx reader of my **Jewish Week** column writes how "pleasantly shocked" he was late one night when he caught **The Villian** on television. There was Kirk Douglas sitting on a wagon playing an organ and singing the entire **Yigdal** hymn in Hebrew.

Tony Curtis

Bernard Schwartz was born June 3, 1926, in The Bronx to an Orthodox family. His father was a struggling immigrant tailor. Curtis told Jack Martin, former **New York Post** columnist: "I avoid Jewish Hollywood not to be different, arrogant, coquettish or cute, but because I choose not to be the type of Jew who runs for his pen instead of his gun. I consider myself a religious Jew and am constantly moved by my background, ancestry and knowledge of whence I came." He starred in such films as **Sweet Smell of Success**, **Houdini**, **Some Like It Hot**, and **Spartacus**.

Jon Voight (left) and Dustin in MIDNIGHT COWBOY.

PHOTO:TIM BOXER

PHOTO:TIM BOXER

DUSTIN HOFFMAN

Born August 8, 1937, in Los Angeles, the actor starred in **The Graduate**, **Midnight Cowboy**, **All The King's Men**, *and* **Kramer vs Kramer** *for which he garnered an Oscar in 1979. His father was an assistant set decorator at Columbia Pictures who later became a furniture designer. Dustin says he grew closer to his mother Lillian in the last days of her life when she had terminal pancreatic cancer. Dustin eagerly jumped at the opportunity when Leonard Goldstein got him to attend a fund-raising dinner for the Israel Cancer Research Fund where a Lillian Hoffman Fellowship was established to enable Israeli scientists to search for a cure for the dreaded disease.*

GOLDIE HAWN

The giddy comedienne of **Laugh-In** *fame breezed past heavy security at the prime minister's office in Jerusalem in November 1986 to tell Yitzhak Shamir of the many trees she had planted in the Holy Land. All the guards on the street and in the corridors reminded her of the two movies she produced and starred in—* **Private Benjamin**, *about a Jewish American Princess in the Army, and* **Protocol**, *a comedy about international diplomacy. In Tel Aviv she layed the cornerstone for a cinematheque, a project initiated by her close friend William Morris agent Stan Kamen, who died recently. The Academy Award winner (for* **Cactus Flower**, *1969) was born November 21, 1945, in Takoma Park, Maryland, a suburb of Washington. Her Jewish mother is Laura Hawn. Her non-Jewish father, musician Edward Rutledge Hawn, is a direct descendant of South Carolina's Edward Rutledge, signer of the Declaration of Independence and later governor.*

Goldie in **tete-a-tete** with Israel's Prime Minister Yitzhak Shamir in Jerusalem.

CAROL KANE

The Emmy winner for **Taxi** and Oscar nominee for **Hester Street** was apprehensive when we met at Moshe Peking, New York's kosher Chinese restaurant. She is a vegatarian but the chef was able to accommodate her nicely. She became a vegetarian at fourteen because "I didn't feel there's a difference seeing people killed and seeing animals killed." She was born June 18, 1952, in Cleveland, Ohio. Her mother, Joy, teaches jazz and plays piano. Her father, Michael, is an architect who designed a temple there. She says she first learned about Judaism when she prepared for **Hester Street** by reading books about the Lower East Side and going to the Jewish Museum. Being an actress helped Carol revive her Jewish self-awareness.

HENRY KISSINGER

The former U.S. Secretary of State was sent by an Israeli prime minister with a list of fifteen proposals to Egyptian President Anwar Sadat. Sadat accepted thirteen. Very pleased, Kissenger returned to report his success to Jerusalem. But the prime minister said, "Why have you betrayed us...again?" Born in Furth, Germany, on May 27, 1923, Kissinger says he barely escaped the Holocaust. He's been watching **Shoah** on tape. "I started seeing it from a sense of duty, then continued seeing it from a sense of destiny. I saw those trains, and I saw my friends being taken to the death camps."

WALTER MATTHAU

Born October 1, 1920, to a dirt-poor family on the Lower East Side, Walter got his first job in the Yiddish theatre, selling soft drinks. Shakespeare was a favorite subject on the Yiddish stage. When Walter was appearing on Broadway, a Yiddish-speaking taxi driver asked, "What are you doing?" Walter replied that he was playing King Lear on Broadway. "Really?" asked the cabbie. "Do you think it would go in English.'

ROBERT MERRILL

The greatest baritone of our time was born Morris Miller on June 4, 1919, in New York. For four years he was a waiter in the Catskills. "I was really a singing waiter," he says. As Merrill Miller, he played the Concord for $25 in 1940. He got 400 times more when he returned as an established star of the Metropolitan Opera. Merrill was married to opera star Roberta Peters — for three months. His current wife is pianist Marion Machno, whom he married in 1945. They have two children, David and Lizanne. He counts Frank Sinatra as his close buddy. In fact, Ol Blue Eyes marvels at Merrill's voice. "I'm jealous," Sinatra says. "Bob sings better and louder than me." Marion retorts, "Don't worry. He still can't be a saloon singer."

PHOTO:TIM BOXER

Frank Sinatra joins Marion and Robert Merrill at Testimonial dinner.

Isaac Stern (left) and Henry Kissinger flank Jerusalem Mayor Teddy Kollek at New York's Lincoln Center.

GEORGE SEGAL

George Segal Jr. was born February 13, 1934, in Great Neck, New York. He is the son of George Sr., a beer dealer, and Fanny Bodkin. He started high school in town but finished at a private Quaker-run school in Bucks County, Pennsylvania. "The most religion I got," he says, "was when I went to Isreal. It's a country ruled by Torah." An El Al official greeted him with "Welcome home." Segal played his banjo for wounded soldiers after which Prime Minister Menachem Begin said, "I don't understand your music, but I like it." Segal's films include **A Touch of Class,** **Who's Afraid of Virginia Woolf?,** *and* **The Owl and the Pussycat.**

TONY RANDALL

He's a non-smoker (and you'd best not light up in his presence), he knows Shakespeare and is an opera buff, and he's a spiffy dresser. In short, he's like Felix Unger, the insufferable character of **The Odd Couple** *for which he was awarded an Emmy in 1975. The elegant performer was born Leonard Rosenberg on February 26, 1920, in Tulsa, Oklahoma. His father Philip was an art dealer who was on the road much of the time, finally leaving for good when Tony was thirteen. Reportedly, Tony commented, "It was pleasant for me—my rival was gone."*

DEBORAH RAFFIN

Born March 13, 1953, in Los Angeles, she made a neat transition from model to actress at eighteen by playing Liv Ullmann's daughter in **Forty Carats**. *Other movie roles followed, including Gregory Peck's production of* **The Dove** *and Jacqueline Susann's* **Once Is Not Enough**. *Her mother, Trudy Marshall, appeared with Laurel and Hardy in* **Dancing Masters**. *Her father, Phil Raffin, operated a meat brokerage firm. She lives with her husband, producer-manager Michael Viner, in Beverly Hills, and in a restored barn in Stowe, Vermont.*

BEVERLY SILLS

Born Belle Miriam Silverman May 25, 1929, in Brooklyn to insurance broker Morris and Shirley (Bahn) Silverman, "Bubbles" grew up to become a brilliant coloratura soprano—who was reputedly for years the highest paid opera singer in the world. She retired at fifty, at the height of her profession, and embarked on a new career as general director of the New York City Opera. The vivacious red-haired diva is inter-married to Boston aristocrat Peter Greenough. Their daughter, Meredith Holden (Muffy) is deaf; their son, Peter Jr. (Bucky) is mentally retarded and epileptic. Beverly works hard on behalf of March of Dimes and Mother's March on Birth Defects.

PHOTO: TIM BOXER

DAVID STEINBERG

Unlike other cerebral comics whose time passed them by, David Steinberg was able to channel his wit and talent in new directions. While Vaughn Meader's rising star went phfft with President Kennedy's untimely demise and David Frye's self-destructed with the Watergate political suicide of Richard Milhouse Nixon, Steinberg—who started with caustic comments on Biblical heroes—tuned up his career by changing gears with the shifting political climate—by seguing into current comedy tinged with social satire.

*He also branched out into films as both an actor **and** a director: His film debut came as Burt Reynolds' lawyer in* **The End;** *he co-starred with Susan Sarandon in* **Something Short of Paradise;** *and in his first feature directed Burt Reynolds in* **Paternity.**

David was born in 1942, the youngest of three children, in my hometown, Winnepeg. His father was a rabbi who—tired of synagogue politics—operated a neighborhood grocery store. Our fathers were friendly because my father also ran a family grocery store. At fifteen David went to the Hebrew Theological College in Skokie, Illinois. I had preceded him there by several years, when the rabbinical school was located on Chicago's West Side. After three years, he went to the Hebrew University in Jerusalem to study Hebrew literature, and returned to earn a Master's in English Literature at the University of Chicago.

His show business career was started in 1962 when he joined SECOND CITY, *the improvisational troupe that launched careers of such notables as Mike Nichols, Elaine May, Alan Arkin, Joan Rivers, Peter Boyle and the late John Belushi. He co-starred with Elliott Gould in Jules Feiffer's* **Little Murders** *on Broadway in 1967. Two years later he returned to the Great White Way in* **Carry Me Back To Morningside Heights** *with Louis Gossett Jr. and Diane Ladd, directed by Sidney Poitier. That same year he began his standup comedy act, integrating his Biblical studies into his routines.*

The upward turn his career took did not impress his mother, Ruth, who lived in Los Angeles. She would say, "The Pulitzer Prize is nice; the Nobel Prize is nice. But if you appear on Johnny Carson Show, that's nachas." Her son not only appeared on America's Number One late-night show, he also began hosting it in Carson's absence.

David's cousin, Morris, is a psychiatrist in New York. While David's career was in an unsteady balance, his parents used to throw up Morris' name every day—as a role model. He was the A student while David was labeled the X. Morris was the prize of the family. When he became not only a doctor but a psychiatrist, it was nirvana.

However, ever since David first appeared on the **Tonight** *show in 1970, Morris name has never been mentioned!*

BARBRA STREISAND

Barbara Joan Streisand dropped a letter from her first name but refused to tinker with her family name, no matter how unglamorous it may sound to some people in Hollywood.

"I don't believe in changing things that you're given," she said on ABC's 20/20. "Something is unnatural about it."

She was born April 24, 1942, in the Williamsburgh section of Brooklyn to Emanuel, an English teacher, and Diana Rosen. Her father died when she was fifteen months old; her mother remarried six years later.

Upon graduation from Erasmus Hall High School in 1959, Barbara left her mother's kosher kitchen to seek fortune as a singer in the coffee houses of Greenwich Village. Later she became a star overnight when she stopped the show with her rendition of Miss Marmelstein in the David Merrick production of **I Can Get It For You Wholesale** *on Broadway.*

Instant success segued into superstardom with her first dramatic leading role as Fanny Brice in **Funny Girl** *on Broadway. The screen version got her an Academy Award in 1968.*

Through innate talent, sheer business acumen and uncompromising integrity, Barbra remains to this day a major force in the world of entertainment.

The fact she is a girl guaranteed Barbra a minimal Jewish religious education (although today's Jewish girls are getting a more intensive religious education than previous generations). Many of the celebrities in the **Hall of Fame** *were exposed to a more intensive Jewish training than was available to Barbra, yet not one has come close to expressing their Jewish emotions in their work as she has done.*

She persevered against all industry attitudes and forged ahead with producing, directing and starring in Isaac Bashevis Singer's **Yentl**. *She told Simcha Dinitz on the cable television program* **Hello Jerusalem**, *"In Hollywood there were people who said, 'Why do you have to make it a Jewish background?' These people were seemingly slightly embarrassed by their Jewish heritage. I was very proud."*

Los Angeles Herald-Examiner *film editor Gregg Kilday, writing in the* **Washington Post**, *uttered a similar assessment of the film colony's mindset: "According to some in Streisand's circle, the very earnestness with which Streisand set out exploring her Jewish roots in* **Yentl** *may have embarrassed some of the more assimilated members of Hollywood's Jewish community."*

The demons that drive (and torment) the Jewish denizens of Beverly Hills do not daunt Barbra, who dotes on her heritage. When film critic Michael Medved helped found the Bay Cities/Pacific Jewish Center, an Orthodox synagogue in Venice, California, Barbra joined Steven Spielberg, Richard Dreyfuss and others in giving a substantial amount of money for the building. She brought her son Jason (by her marriage to Elliott Gould) here for his bar mitzvah. The rabbi, David Lapin, had her come to the Hebrew classes with her son.

She also donated $50,000 in 1981, to establish a Streisand Center for Jewish Cultural Arts at Hillel House on the UCLA campus.

Mike Burstyn finds himself sandwiched between Brooke Shields and Elizabeth Taylor at VARIETY CLUB affair in Tel Aviv.

ELIZABETH TAYLOR

Contrary to widespread belief, the most glamorous convert to Judaism did not do it for the sake of her husband Mike Todd—whom she loved very much. In fact, the flamboyant producer, born Avrom Goldbogen, dissauded his lovely wife from embracing his religion. He told her that conversion was a serious matter and that she should study the subject before making such a difficult decision.

After he died in a 1958 plane crash, Elizabeth took up with Eddie Fisher—when again she felt the longing for the Jewish faith. At the time they were living together as love birds in Los Angeles—waiting for Eddie's divorce from Debbie Reynolds. One day he brought home a pile of books on Judaica and they both delved into the history of his people and the meaning of Jewish customs and laws. The more she read, the more convinced Elizabeth became that it was right to convert.

On March 3, 1959, she was converted in a Reform ceremony by Rabbi Max Nussbaum at Temple Israel in Hollywood. She took the name Elisheba ("Oath of God"), the Hebrew form of Elizabeth.

That same year Elizabeth and Eddie were married at Temple Bath Shalom in Las Vegas. The ceremony was conducted by Rabbi Bernard Cohen, with assistance from Rabbi Nussbaum.

While Elizabeth has been married seven times to six men, the love of her life remains Mike Todd, the one husband she did not divorce. She continues to embrace his faith and supports Jewish interests such as the Simon Wiesenthal Center in Los Angeles and the Hebrew University in Jerusalem.

The beautiful star sparked a sensation when she toured Israel in 1983, escorted by New York journalist Ray Errol Fox. The temperature was so hot that she was rushed to hospital for oxygen. Ariel Sharon sent two cars to bring her to his farm. On the way to the farm, the car was involved in a three-car collision. Elizabeth suffered a broken finger and neck whiplash — Fox sustained two broken ribs. The actress canceled a trip to the Lebanese border. The bus assigned to take her there was blown up.

"You saw how safe it is to be with her!" says Zev Bufman. He produced **Private Lives** on Broadway which starred Elizabeth and then-husband Richard Burton.

At the Western Wall, she wrote a prayer on a piece of paper which she inserted into a crack in the Wall. The message was simple: "Peace to all men."

The Variety Club invited her to reign at the DIPLOMATS BALL on a New Year's Eve at the Tel Aviv Hilton. In the middle of the party, Cannon Films' chief Menahem Golan brought Brooke Shields into the room. She had been filming **Sahara** in the country. Mike Burstyn, who starred on Broadway in **Barnum** and in Israel in the **Kuni Lemel** movies, was the master of ceremonies. He called on Brooke to join Elizabeth in cutting the festive cake.

"El;izabeth turned to me and gave me such a cold look,," Burstyn recalls. "It was the first time it snowed in the Hilton Ballroom."

The volatile, lavender-eyed actress was born February 27, 1932, in London, England. The most glamorous career of the silver screen was launched when she appeared as an angelic child star in **National Velvet** and got two Oscars (**Butterfield 8** and **Who's Afraid of Virginia Woolf?**) — together with those six husbands (Nicky Hilton, Michael Wilding, Mike Todd, Eddie Fisher, Richard Burton [twice] and the politician John Warner).

As Frank Sinatra announced at a FRIARS roast: "Tonight we talk about the lives and loves of Elizabeth Taylor. Relax, folks, we're going to be here a long time."

Sinatra noted that Elizabeth got married seven times — and got richer by decrees.

Following on in the same light-hearted vein, Red Buttons allowed as how he was delighted to be at a roast with Elizabeth because, "My father was a tailor."

PHOTO:TIM BOXER

ELI WALLACH

When Eli Wallach first went to Israel with his wife Anne Jackson ("a lapsed Catholic") and agent Peter Witte, a street vendor in Bethlehem tried to sell him some postcards. Eli declined saying he'll take his own pictures.

The vendor pointed towards Anne and said, "I'll give you ten sheep and ten camels for her."

As Eli reflected on a proper response, Peter broke in: "Take it—I get ten percent."

*Eli was born December 7, 1915, in Brooklyn to Abraham and Bertha (Schorr) Wallach. Unlike his brother and two sisters who became teachers, Eli became an actor. Discharged from the Army Medical Corps after World War II, he performed in Tennessee Williams' **This Property Is Condemned** in New York, playing opposite Anne Jackson–they married in 1948.*

That he is one of our best actors was shown early in his career when he was awarded a TONY *in 1951 as **Best Supporting Actor** for his role as the Sicilian lover opposite Maureen Stapleton in Tennessee Williams' **The Rose Tattoo**. He went on to distinguish himself in other stage plays (such as **Luv** and **Rhinoceros** in 1961 and a 1978 Toronto production of **The Diary of Anne Frank** with his wife and daughter (Roberta) plus many motion pictures (including **The Tiger Makes Out** in 1973 and **The Sentinel** in 1976).*

LESLIE ANN WARREN

As a fifteen-year-old beauty she wanted to leave home to tour in a Broadway musical. She had sneaked out of the house to go to an audition for the national company of **Bye Bye Birdie**. *Her parents, like typical Jewish parents, said, "No way." It was more important for her to finish high school. She decided on a life in the theatre – after high school, that is. A year later, Leslie got her first Broadway role as a flirtatious hussy in* **110 in the Shade**. *At the same time, during the day, she portrayed a virginal Cinderella in the television musical – Rogers and Hammerstein's version of* **Cinderella**. *She got an Oscar nomination as the flaky floozy in* **Victor/Victoria** *in 1982.*

Leslie enjoyed playing Anna Friedman, the Jewish matriarch of an immigrant family at the turn of the century in the NBC miniseries **Evergreen**, *based on Belva Plain's novel. She doesn't necessarily identify with the character. "I don't share her passivity. I don't sit back and shut up."*

The actress was born in 1949, in New York. Her father, William Warrenoff, came from Russia and shortened the family name before Leslie was born. He is currently in real estate in Los Angeles.

Her mother is the former singer Carol Verblow, who came from England although her mother was from Russia. Leslie was brought up Reform although her grandmother was Orthodox.

Leslie teams with Ian McShane and Armand Assante in NBC's EVERGREEN.

SHELLEY WINTERS

"I've got the market cornered on Jewish mothers and whores," Shelley once told **Newsday**.

Indeed, she hasn't done badly portraying Jewish women. She was the typical Jewish mother in **Next Stop, Greenwich Village**, **Minnie's Boys** *and, of course,* **The Diary of Anne Frank**. *In* **The Poseidon Adventure** *(which netted her an Oscar nomination) she and Jack Albertson played Jewish grandparents on their way to visit their daughter and grandchild in Israel when they are engulfed by a tidal wave.*

PHOTO: TIM BOXER

Nevertheless, she is sick and tired of playing Jewish mothers all the time. She told me she's "trying to break that image of the Jewish woman. All I'm offered is the Jewish-mother role. I feel it's something I have to play down. In the last twenty years, I've been offered only Jewish mother roles."

She resents the image Hollywood had molded for the Jewish mothers which she has been forced to portray for so many years.

"Producers feel being a Jewish woman is a yenta. On the Tonight Show, David Susskind called me a 'momumental yenta.' I have to stop this image. It's a serious career problem. Maureen Stapleton has been getting all the parts I should be getting," she adds with a lusty laugh.

These sentiments about Hollywood pigeon-holing her as a Jewish yenta has nothing to do with her true feelings about Jewishness.

"I'm proud to be Jewish," she affirms. "Everybody knows I'm Jewish. I was just honored by Hadassah."

In fact, she is a confirmed Zionist and an active member of WRITERS AND ARTISTS FOR PEACE IN THE MIDDLE EAST. She simply wants to broaden her scope on the screen and play characters that have long been denied her because narrow minded Hollywood producers see her as the stereotypical Jewish mother.

She was born Shirley Schrift on August 18, 1923, in East St. Louis,Illiniois, to fashion designer Johann Schrift and opera singer Rose Schrift. Eleven years later they moved to Brooklyn. She started out as a dress model in the Garment Center. When she did summer stock she changed her name to Shelley Winter (her mother's maiden name) and then Winters for the movies.

Her first real success (and Oscar nomination) came with the role of a tramp waitress who is murdered by Ronald Colman in the 1948 motion picture **A Double Life**. Her loves are well documented. She married textile salesman Mack Paul Mayer in 1942 and divorced him in 1948.

In 1951 she was engaged to Farley Granger, but they never married. Earl Wilson asked, "Why not?"

"It was a matter of life or death," she replied heatedly.

"What do you mean?"

"We would have killed each other."

The following year the Brooklyn bombshell dumped Granger to marry Italian movie idol Vittorio Gassman. They have a daughter, Vittoria (Tory). The marriage ended in a shambles.

"We were never two people in love," she reportedly said. "I was in love with him...and he was in love with him."

She essayed a third marital fling with another Italian-rooted actor, Anthony Franciosa. Now she is enjoying the single life.

Shelley was victorious in the 1959 Oscar sweepstakes when she was voted BEST SUPPORTING ACTRESS for **The Diary of Anne Frank**. She donated the gold statuette to the ANNE FRANK MUSEUM in Amsterdam. She copped a second Oscar in the same category in 1965 for **A Patch of Blue**.

Peter, Paul and Mary.

PETER YARROW

"Many of my ideas are Jewish-based," says the Jewish third of Peter, Paul and Mary. He was born May 31, 1938, in New York. Peter's Russian father taught Hebrew, then became an attorney. Yet Peter was brought up on Ethical Culture until his mother remarried after which he went to Central Synagogue — the Reform temple on the East Side where he was confirmed. He is separated from film producer, Mary Beth McCarthy, niece of Sen. Eugene McCarthy. They have a teenage son, Christopher, and a daughter, Bethany. Peter does a lot of benefits, especially for his son's public school and for Ansche Chesed Synagogue on the West Side.

The folk singing trio went to Israel in 1983 where they planted saplings in a Jewish National Fund forest outside Jerusalem. Then they gave a concert for 10,000 people at the foot of Mount Zion. Among the many songs was a Chanukah song written by Peter, who told the audience how important his Jewishness was to him:

Light one candle for the Macabbee children
 with thanks that their light didn't die
Light one candle for the pain they endured
 when their right to exist was denied
Light one candle for the terrible sacrifice
 justice and freedom demand
But light one candle for the wisdom to know
 when the peacemaker's time is at hand.

CELEBRITIES
WHO ARE
HALF JEWISH

Statistics indicate that fifty percent of Jewish people marry outside the faith. In 1960 the rate of intermarriage was ten percent. This attrition of the Jewish population in America has long been punctuated by prime examples in the Hollywood community. The Southern California tribal rite of mate swapping easily infected the many Jewish members of the show biz colony. In a conscious effort to appeal to mainstream Anglo-Saxon sensibilities, the Jewish thespians switched religions as easily as names, noses, speech and eating habits.

Thus a new generation of "half-Jews" has been spawned. The progeny of these mixed marriages sometimes indentify with the mother's faith, sometimes with the father's. According to *halachah*, of course, if the mother is Gentile then the offspring also is non-Jewish. Orthodox law ascribes religious lineage to the maternal line. (Reform and Reconstructionist rabbis recognize any child in a mixed marriage—no matter which parent is Jewish—as a Jewish child.)

Essentially, then, there is no such thing as a "half-Jew." Orthodox edict ascribes Jewishness to the child of a Jewish mother, not to the child of a Gentile mother. Reform ruling accepts both into the fold.

Official codes notwithstanding, many celebrities who had a Jewish father and a Gentile mother still prefer to think of themselves as members of the Chosen People. There is even an organization, *Paraveh* which has been created to deal with the identity crisis that ensues among intermarriage children. *Paraveh* is the term ascribed to food products (such as fruit and vegetables) that are neither meat nor dairy, and can be eaten with both. In other words—neutral.

Phoebe stars with Willie Aames in PARADISE.

PHOEBE CATES

Born July 16, 1963 in New York to producer-director Joe Cates, whose real name was Katz. When he first sold a radio script to J. Walter Thompson ad agency in 1948, they did not want an ethnic name on the credits so they changed his name to Kates. Phoebe starred in **Paradise, Fast Times at Ridgemont High** *and* **Gremlins** *on the big screen and in the* **Lace** *miniseries. She's dating Kevin Kline, whose Jewishness also stems only from his father.*

JOAN COLLINS

Bitch goddess Alexis Colby of **Dynasty** *has a Jewish father, Joe Collins, a theatrical agent in England. Joan, who calls herself "a well-brought up half-Jewish girl," was born on May 23, 1923, in London.*

JAMIE LEE CURTIS

An established name in the horror flick genre, Jamie is the daughter of actor Tony Curtis (born Bernie Schwartz of The Bronx) and actress Janet Leigh.

CARRIE FISHER

The intriguing Princess Leia of the money record-setting **Star Wars** *is the daughter of Eddie Fisher and Debbie Reynolds.*

ROBERT DE NIRO

*The Academy Award winner (*BEST SUPPORTING ACTOR *as Vito Corleone in* **The Godfather, Part 11** *and* BEST ACTOR *as Jake La Motta in* **Raging Bull***) is the son of two Greenwich Village artists, a Jewish mother and Italian father. He was born on August 17, 1943, in New York.*

DEAD END KIDS: **(left to right)** Leo Gorcey, Billy Halop, Huntz Hall, Bobby Jordan, Gabriel Dell and Bernard Punsley.

PHOTO:PICTORIAL PARADE

LEO GORCEY

Slip Mahoney of the BOWERY BOYS *movies had a Jewish father, Bernard Gorcey, a comedian who played candy store owner Louis Dombrowski in those flicks. Leo, who died in 1969 at age 52, also played monkey-faced Spit in the* **Dead End Kids** *films.*

PHOTO:TIM BOXER

Cary Grant with Nina Boxer, my wife, at a board meeting of FABERGE where both worked.

CARY GRANT

After making 72 films in 32 years, the silver-haired heartthrob to millions of women became a goodwill ambassador for FABERGE. My wife Nina, who was secretary to the late Harris Sobol, a vice president of the cosmetic company, reports that the sophisticated sauve film star always charmed the ladies when he arrived for board of directors meetings when the firm was still under the private tutelage of business executive-composer-movie produce George Barrie. The witty and stylish leading man died a trouper on November 29, 1986, in the Mississippi River town of Davenport, Iowa, where he was rehearsing for "A Conversation with Cary Grant." The legendary star of the silver screen was born Archibald Alexander Leach on January 18, 1904, in Bristol, England. His half-Jewish father died a drunk, his mentally-disturbed mother was institutionalized, and he ran away from home at age thirteen — to become a shining light of the Hollywood star system.

JOHN HOUSEMAN

MICHAEL LANDON

Distinguished writer-producer-director-actor, Oscar-winning star of **The Paper Chase**, *was born Jean Haussmann September 22, 1902, in Bucharest, Romania, to a Jewish grain speculator and Welsh-Irish mother.*

Star and co-producer of NBC's **Little House on the Prarie** *and star-executive producer of* **Highway to Heaven** *was born Eugene Orowitz October 31, 1937, in Forest Hills, N.Y., to a Jewish father Sam and Catholic mother.*

PAUL NEWMAN

The blue-eyed actor was born January 26, 1925, in Cleveland. His Jewish father, Arthur Newman, ran a sporting goods store. His Catholic mother became a Christian Scientist. He calls himself a Jew. Married to actress Joanne Woodward, Paul was Oscar-nominated for **Cat On A Hot Tin Roof** *(1958),* **The Hustler** *(1961),* **Hud** *(1963),* **Cool Hand Luke** *(1967),* **Absence of Malice** *(1981), and* **The Verdict** *(1982).*

PHOTO:FRANK EDWARDS/FOTOS INTERNATIONAL

ROMAN POLANSKI

Film director and husband of the late Sharon Tate, Polanski was born August 18, 1933, in Paris of Jewish father and Polish Catholic mother. Both perished in Auschwitz. In his autobiography **Roman**, *Polanski says his mother "was only part Jewish." He most recently directed Walter Matthau in* **Pirates** *for Cannon Films.*

JOHN RUBINSTEIN

Composer and actor, who starred with Jack Warden in **Crazy Like A Fox** *on TV, was born December 8, 1946, to Jewish pianist Arthur Rubinstein and Polish Catholic mother. John says he is a proud half-Jew."*

PHOTO:COLUMBIA PICTURES TELEVISION

JANE SEYMOUR

Born Joyce Frankenberg on February 15, 1951, in England to a Polish Jewish physician, John Frankenberg, who escaped from Nazi Germany with his Dutch wife.

PAULA STEWART

Singer-actress, ex-wife of composer Burt Bacharach and comedian Jack Carter, had a German Jewish father and Irish mother.

Paula Stewart (**left**) and film comedienne Barbara Nichols at film premier of WHAT's NEW PUSSYCAT?" in New York.

CELEBRITIES
WHO THINK
THEY'RE JEWISH
BUT AREN'T SURE

ROBERT CULP

The man who starred in such films as *Bob & Carol & Ted & Alice* and the NBC series *I Spy* (with Bill Cosby from 1965 to 1968) is honest, if nothing else. Oh, he was quite sincere when he decided to convert to Judaism in 1960. But he always felt like the kid with his nose pressed to the candy store window. He saw himself as an outsider. So after a few years of attending services on the Sabbath and the High Holy Days with his then wife, Nancy Wilner, he let go his Jewish wife and his newfound Jewish faith.

Robert was born on August 16, 1930, in Berkeley, California. He was not raised with any sense of religious belief. The question simply never came up. His ancestors were western pioneer stock. "My grandmother's family was Methodist," Robert says, "but after coming west in covered wagons she became Episcopalian. She was married for fifty years. My grandfather—you couldn't get him into a church. Churchgoing or thinking about religion was not part of his makeup."

Through an intellectual process, Robert concluded that for all the questions in the universe, Judaism provided the best answers.

"I began to perceive that while the law of the entire western world proceeds from Roman law, Roman law came from Jewish law. Ergo, what we have that is so sacred, in terms of documents among men, proceeds from Jewish law. That's interesting. What does that mean?

"Does that mean some kind of mix of the Talmud and Torah? The answer is yes."

Upon forther reflection, Robert became impressed with the power of the melting pot of the United States, breaking down its various ethnic components into a common ordinary soup of Americans. Much like enzymes breaking down food matter in a living organism. This acculturation worked for every nationality and ethnic group except one.

Spied at the opening of Ritz Carlton Hotel in Laguna Niguel, California, Robert Culp and his lovely wife Candace.

"The minority we call Jews," Robert observed, "do not simply assimilate as fast as the Judaic fathers fear they are disappearing. They're not. There is something intrinsically Jewish that remains generation after generation, whereas in the Irish, Italian, Polish—okay, a certain ethnicity remain, but most of it is leavened. Most of it is softened; the edges are blurred away.

"Not so the Jews.

"There is a problem with people who have been brought up in this social and ethical format called Judaism that does not easily break down. There is tremendous resistance to it.

"For those reasons, I had such a high regard for that ethic which is Old Testament that I said, 'Gee, I feel at home here. I really feel at home.'"

He married Nancy in 1956. She had a large, extended family in Baltimore, which they visited often. Robert felt closer to them than he did to her parents, "with whom I still had some difficult problems." But he was doing well as an actor. He was starring as Hoby Gilman in *Trackdown*, a western that aired on CBS from 1957 to 1959. He played a mythical Texas Ranger. This was the only western that had the official approval of the State of Texas and the Rangers. He was the delight of Nancy's relatives because he was in show business, doing terrific, and a star.

"Some of them I really adored. Her aunt, who was the *alte mama* of the family, was nuts about me and I was nuts about her. They were all proud of me. So I felt approval."

It was while filming *Trackdown*, and living in their first little house they bought in the San Fernando Valley, that Robert decided to take formal lessons in Judaism at Temple Beth El. He went to classes for several months, then went through a conversion ceremony.

"I really don't know what in the world you would call it. You may as well call it a *bris*. We said a few words one to another. Then the rabbi presented me with a little scroll, which has no really intrinsic value, but it meant something to me.

"The point was, I had assimilated a certain amount of knowledge and Jewishness, essentially, and I had gained the respect, if not the admiration, of my in-laws.

"Nancy's father had had a terrible time with her married name. Although she never pressed me, it was time for this. It was my initiative altogether."

Although Nancy would never press him, she was delighted he had taken the step. It offered a platform on which to raise their three sons and one daughter.

The marriage lasted ten years. Even before the breakup, Robert began entertaining doubts about the veracity of his action. He attended synagogue on the High Holy Days year after year, and year after year he continued to feel like the kid with his nose pressed against the candy store window. He felt outside looking in.

Celebrating the High Holy Days is one of the things that is so strong that it does not break down in the American melting pot. It is the product of thousands of years of being a Jew.

"It wasn't mine," Robert felt. "I didn't possess that. That I couldn't have because I hadn't been born into it."

He found it strange that Judaism should be so different from other religions. The essence of Catholicism is you do not have to be born into it. You are simply blessed or anointed into it.

"Anybody can do it, folks. Aha, not so a Jew. You are born a Jew.

"If you want to adopt the concept of becoming a Jew, it is an extraordinary, time-consuming effort. And then you might not do it. That is the reason why the effort to do so is held in scant approval, kind of looked at sideways, with a certain skepticism, by Jews who know better.

"This is not some kind of reverse discrimination. It is not that at all. It is just that it's damn difficult. Human beings, unless they are born into something, do tend to feel like outsiders.

"That feeling is magnified when you don't understand the language, which is very basic, at the heart of the Jewish experience. Here are the players, here are the moments of holy togetherness, and you don't understand the language.

"You can't slide by: Well, it doesn't matter if I don't actually know the Hebrew anymore, because I know Yiddish. A Jew could say that. I could not say that."

There was a hole in the fabric. When Robert and his wife grew separate from each other, the hole got bigger. Regretfully, he let go of the fabric.

"But I'm still proud of it," he says. "I'm proud of that period of time in my life and what it gave me, which was a great spiritual solidity."

Where does he stand now on religion?

The same I started with—none. That's not quite true. But it's not formalized. I absolutely believe in a Supreme Being. When you look at the fact that all of the world's great minds have all come to the conclusion that it is impossible, all this stuff in the universe is really impossible—as random as it appears—you finally wind up with the mind of God.

"I tend to find the formalization in all of the world's religions still a bit wanting in imagination. But isn't that okay, also, because we have finite imagination, and God doesn't? Judaism allows for that. Isn't that wonderful? All of the other religions don't."

We were sitting in the living room of his Beverly Hills home. Robert, dressed in white Bermuda shorts and a white sport shirt, reflected for a moment. Then he looked up and said, "It's interesting. I have always found that I am able to converse on this subject with a Jew, especially someone trained, such as a rabbi. It's always fascinating conversation. And I don't dare walk on those grounds with anybody else on the so-called Christian ethic. You just don't walk over there."

I assured Robert that the Talmud consists of a cast of characters posing conflicting views from beginning to end. The Talmud, the core of the Jewish religion, is one long, seemingly endless, debate. But everyone seems to reach a common conclusion.

He smiled. "Basically I was right to start with," he said.

ALI MACGRAW

Her identity crisis took hold during the year she filmed the TV superseries, *The Winds of War,* the chronicle of the beginnings of World War II and the Holocaust, which aired in 1983 on ABC. She played Natalie Jastrow, an American Jew who goes to Florence to study with her uncle and gets caught up in the Nazi maelstrom.

She told me all about it at a party *Interview* threw in her honor at the Limelight in Atlanta. She was the current cover girl of Andy Warhol's magazine. We sat on a black leather couch in a relatively quiet corner of the disco and conversed for an hour. At one point she got hiccups and, while she held her breath, I patted her on the back. It worked.

We know she was born in New York on April 1, 1939, and brought up in Bedford Village, New York. Her first job out of Wellesley College was assistant to Diana Vreeland at *Harper's Bazaar.* She became a much sought after cover model, with a rare combination of intelligence and beauty. Her acting breakthrough came with the role of Brenda Patimkin, the quintessential Jewish American Princess, in Philip Roth's *Goodbye, Columbus* (1969). At first she was turned down because they said she wasn't the Jewish type. A few months later they called her back. Following that she played an Italian girl, the doomed Jenny Cavilleri, in the piercing *Love Story* (1971).

She was married three times. First was just out of college, for a brief time. Second to producer Bob Evans. Then to Steve McQueen, her co-star in *The Getaway.* Bob is Jewish and the father of her son Joshua.

The question lingers: "Who am I?"

"I want to know who I am," she tells me. "I was brought up in New York as an Episcopalian. I believe there was Jewish blood on my mother's side. Grandfather Maurice Klein came from Budapest at age fourteen and worked in a sweatshop here.

"To me it says, Jewish family.

"It's disturbing that here I am, a grownup, and I have no idea who I am. Everybody who can tell me is dead."

Making this seven-part TV miniseries affected her in profound ways that she was not prepared for.

"We filmed the exodus from Poland," she said, recalling the scene of thousands of Jews fleeing Warsaw in the face of the German onslaught.

"I escaped in a car with Topol at the wheel. When they called a lunch break, I couldn't join the cast to eat and chat. I went off by myself...and cried. I couldn't break the mood. For me, it was really happening.

"There's an Orthodox wedding scene, very moving. After the ceremony and joyous dancing, the Nazis came and strafed the village. I found it absolutely devastating.

Intriguing Ali MacGraw spills the "secrets" of her heart to author at movie bash in the LIMELIGHT *in Atlanta, Georgia.*

"I was in Yugoslavia for a year and a half. All that time, between takes, I was in a trance. At the end I had participated in one of the most important things in my life. Dan Curtis, the producer-director who is Jewish, spent four years of his life putting this whole thing together. I'm very lucky to be in it."

During a break, Topol took Ali to Zagreb to see some of the actors in the film put on a production of *The Dybbuk.* They were members of the Polish Yiddish theater. They spoke Russian, Polish, Yiddish, but Topol translated for Ali.

Ali was so affected by Herman Wouk's *The Winds of War* that when the filming was completed, she found herself questioning her identity.

For the first time in her charmed life she began asking, "Who am I?"

CELEBRITIES YOU ALWAYS THOUGHT WERE JEWS *BUT AREN'T*

MICHAEL CAINE

Put James Cagney and Michael Caine in the same room and you might get scintillating conversation going—in Yiddish! And they are not even Jewish!

Cagney grew up in Hell's Kitchen and learned Yiddish on the streets. He uses *mama loshen* in his 1932 movie *Taxi*. A cop asks, "What part of Ireland did your folks come from?" and Cagney replies, "Delancey Street, denk yew."

What is Michael Caine's excuse for being mistaken as Jewish most of his life? The star of *Dressed to Kill, Sleuth, Alfie* and *The Ipcress File* was born Maurice Joseph Micklewhite on March 14, 1933, in a London slum. The young cockney attended the only nearby school, Hackney Downs Grammar School, which he says was a private Jewish institution. He was one of twelve Protestants there. Harold Pinter was graduated from that school.

"I got thrown out at the end," Michael recalled. "We were a rough lot. But I can carry a conversation in Yiddish."

His father was a Catholic fish market porter; his mother a Protestant charwoman. He belongs to the Church of England. His wife Shakira Baksh, a former Miss Guyana in a Miss World beauty pageant, is a Muslim. Their daughter's Christian name is Natasha, her Muslim name Halima. As Michael tells it, "Bob Hope said I wasn't sure if there was a God, but if there is, I didn't want to lose out on a technicality."

Father gave him good advice: "Never be in a job where you can be replaced by a machine." So after working at the Billingsgate fish market and in a laundry, he became an actor. With the proliferation of science fiction pictures where the hero is 3CPO, maybe he is in the wrong business after all!

ANTHONY NEWLEY

Despite my querying Anthony Newley on three different occasions in the last seven years about the veracity of the rumor that he might be Jewish, he continues to deny it. During a rehearsal for his major Saturday night stage show at the Concord Hotel in Kiamesha Lake, New York, he took a break to set the record straight for me.

"I have no religion," he affirmed.

That is not satisfactory. I pressed on. Since the Jews constitute a culture and civilization, you may profess atheism, agnosticism or even Christian Science, and still be counted among the Jewish people.

"I'm not Jewish," he declared with finality, and went on to explain.

"My mother's mother was Jewish. My father's mother was Irish. My father was raised in the Church of England, if anything. I was brought up in the Anglican Church. I did not have the benefit of being raised a Jew. Intellectually, I am a Zen Buddhist."

Since according to *halacha* (Talmudic law), whether one is a Jew or not is determined by the mother's side, Tony is technically a Jew. But he denies it.

Nonetheless, the belief is widespread that he is a Jew. Not only is he listed in several books of Jewish lists, but the prestigious *Celebrity Register* has also chosen to list him

among the descendants of Abraham, Isaac and Jacob, to wit: "A cockney Jew born in the East End of London, 24 September 1931."

His second wife was Joan Collins, whose father was Jewish. He has two children from that marriage. His current wife is Dareth who is Catholic, and they have two children. "I am a family man, a *heimischeh* boy," as he puts it.

Newley established a worldwide reputation when he wrote, directed and starred in *Stop the World, I Want to Get Off*." With Jewish writer Stanley Ralph Ross, he has co-authored a play called *Chaplin* which he hopes to bring to Broadway.

He tells me that Charlie Chaplin "was a mixture of everything, including Jewish." Chaplin wanted to play Jesus Christ in a film. At a production meeting, according to Newley, Chaplin got up and stated, "I'm perfect for the role of Jesus Christ—I'm Jewish."

Despite Newley's protests that he is not Jewish, my Talmudic authority, Rabbi Ephraim Buchwald of the renowned Lincoln Square Synagogue in Manhattan, maintains that Jewish law regards Newley as a Jew. He can thank his maternal grandmother for that.

PHOTO:TIM BOXER

Jerry Orbach

Although his father was Jewish, Jerry took up his mother's faith. She was Polish Catholic. Jerry was born in the Bronx on October 20, 1935, and raised in Waukegan, Illinois. His father Leon Orbach managed restaurants.

"My father's ancestors," he said, "were Sephardic who left Spain during the Inquisition and settled in Baden Baden, Germany. They changed their name to Orbach, meaning 'city by the sea.'"

After studying drama at Northwestern University, Jerry got his first break when Joel Grey's wife Jo helped him become an understudy in *The Threepenny Opera*. He was in *The Fantasticks, Carnival, Promises, Promises* (for which he won a Tony Award), and *Forty-second Street*.

Jerry may not be Jewish but he knows some funny stories. A writer from a Yiddish paper was assigned to the science beat. Instead of relating dry facts and figures, he put a little something of himself into his science dispatches. He wrote an article about the sun, radiation and temperature. "At the core of the sun the temperature exceeds 400,000 C." To which he added, "Here the heat is unbearable."

ROD STEIGER

Who could fault you for thinking Rod Steiger is Jewish? Even he is not sure at times. He was born Rodney Steven Steiger on April 14, 1925, in Westhampton, New York. He grew up Lutheran in a Jewish area of Newark, New Jersey.

"I was the only Gentile in a Jewish neighborhood, so I think of myself as Jewish very often," he told me. "When I was six or seven years old, I would light the stoves every Friday after sundown in some of the Jewish homes. I got five cents for lighting the gas for the women. They called me a *Shabbos goy*."

We were sitting in the Russian Tea Room, favorite watering hole of New York's film stars. He wore a fashionable dark-blue Greek sailor cap, not to emulate an Orthodox Jew who keeps his head covered—"I'm agnostic"—but to cover a balding dome. He did not put on his toupee that day.

People have been taking Rod for Jewish ever since he vividly portrayed a Jew with a German accent in *The Pawnbroker*. He is such a splendid actor, he convinced countless admirers that he must be Jewish. He got $25,000 for doing that movie role—"Nobody would do the story of

Non-Jew Rod Steiger pulls off startlingly authentic performance as a Hassidic rebbe in THE CHOSEN.

an old Jew"—and he earned critical acclaim for his powerful performance. In the highly publicized picture *The
Chosen*, he essayed the role of a Hasidic rabbi complete
with white flowing beard, *shtreimel* and the traditional
black frock coat.

"In *The Chosen*, I took less than I would normally get,"
he said, "because there are parts that are an adventure,
that make you want to get up in the morning, that make
you want to be proud to try to do something. I am an
actor. Life without a challenge is dead, monotony, it's not
of interest to me. In this picture I have a challenge.

"This is the first time I've had this Jewish accent. I picked
it up in a butcher shop in Manhattan. I heard this butcher
talking to these Jewish ladies. They were about sixty or
seventy years old. I got into the conversation with them.
We all talked with this Jewish accent. Then the butcher
went into Yiddish and I had to confess I couldn't speak
Yiddish. I didn't tell him I was an actor.

"I went to Crown Heights in Brooklyn where I listened
to Hasidic people. I went to their service and saw their
great leader, Rabbi Schneerson. I didn't meet him; I just
watched.

"I have been thinking. Having come from a broken
home and not having known my father—I've been on my
own since I was twelve—I missed something. All of a
sudden, I'm thinking it must be nice to have a real family."

A year after he was born, Rod's mother divorced and
remarried. He grew up a loner. He left high school at sixteen and lied about his age to enlist in the Navy during
World War II.

A versatile leading man, Rod made his mark in the title
role of the original live television production of *Marty* in
1953. Innumerable acting jobs followed, but his memo-
rable performances include the young gangster in the hard-
hitting *On the Waterfront* (1954), for which he got an
Academy Award nomination, and the redneck sheriff in
the powerful *In the Heat of the Night* (1967), which earned
him an Oscar as Best Actor.

As for his desire for a real family, he tried three times, in vain. He married actress Sally Gracie in 1952, British actress Claire Bloom in 1959, and racing handicapper Sherry Nelson in 1973. His union with the Jewish Bloom gave him his only child, Anna Justine, a dramatic soprano.

Looking over the vibrant lifestyle in the Lubavitch community of Crown Heights, Rod realized there was a terrible void in his own life. "Here," he mused, "I see the camaraderie among these people and I see how they treat their children. I see the family quality. I begin to think maybe I could have had more children. Just for the family spirit alone."

One thing he has never lost is his delightful sense of humor. Remember when Sophia Loren hosted a television special on Rome, and Elizabeth did one on London, their respective hometowns? Well, Rod would like to do one on Newark, which he calls "crossroads of a million housing projects." Frank Sinatra, he suggests, could do Hoboken. And David Steinberg, I propose, could do Winnipeg, our hometown.

GLOSSARY

alef beis gimel   first three letters of Hebrew alphabet

al chet   litany of sins recited on Yom Kippur

alte mama   old mother (term of endearment)

bar mitzvah   synagogue ceremony on boy's 13th birthday obligating him to fulfill all commandments of Torah

bat mitzvah   synagogue ceremony for girl's coming-of-age

bimah   platform where cantor stands

Breishis   Genesis

bris   circumcision

bulvahn   gross

challah   bread baked specially for Shabbos